# MOTHER GOOSE
# Unplucked

The
Not-So-Good
Fairy →

**Maple Tree Press Inc.**
51 Front Street East, Suite 200, Toronto, Ontario M5E 1B3
www.mapletreepress.com

Distributed in Canada by Raincoast Books
9050 Shaughnessy Street, Vancouver, British Columbia V6P 6E5

Distributed in the United States by Publishers Group West
1700 Fourth Street, Berkeley, California 94710

**Dedication**
For Anne, Victoria, and Sheba

**Cataloguing in Publication Data**
Becker, Helaine, 1961–
       Mother Goose unplucked : crazy comics, zany activities, nutty facts, and other twisted takes on childhood favorites / Helaine Becker ; illustrated by Claudia Dávila.

ISBN-13: 978-1-897066-83-6 (bound) / ISBN-10: 1-897066-83-X (bound)
ISBN-13: 978-1-897066-84-3 (pbk.) / ISBN-10: 1-897066-84-8 (pbk.)

       I. Dávila, Claudia  II. Title.

PS8553.E295532M67 2007            jC813'.6            C2006-904159-8

Design & illustrations: Claudia Dávila

We acknowledge the financial support of the Canada Council for the Arts, the Ontario Arts Council, the Government of Canada through the Book Publishing Industry Development Program (BPIDP), and the Government of Ontario through the Ontario Media Development Corporation's Book Initiative for our publishing activities.

ONTARIO ARTS COUNCIL
CONSEIL DES ARTS DE L'ONTARIO

Printed in China

A       B       C       D       E       F

# MOTHER GOOSE Unplucked

## Crazy Comics, Zany Activities, Nutty Facts, & Other Twisted Takes on Childhood Favorites

WRITTEN BY
**HELAINE BECKER**

ILLUSTRATED BY
**CLAUDIA DÁVILA**

MAPLE TREE PRESS

# CONTENTS

# Mother Goose Gets Down on the Farm

# A Trip to Ye Olde Town

# ONce UPON

BONG BONG BONG BONG BONG BONG BONG BONG BONG BONG

Once upon a time, there was a remarkably strange land named Happilyeverafter. It was inhabited by high-strung pigs and long-winded wolves, industrious fairies and crafty dragons, kings, queens, princesses, princes, pipers, and paupers. Houses were made out of gingerbread, shoes out of glass, and pies out of blackbirds. Or so they say....

But what's the *real* story of Humpty Dumpty? Why on Earth did Little Bo Peep keep losing her sheep? And what about all that fairy tale magic? Did it really work? And if so, could *you* learn how to turn a duckling into a swan, make a magic wand that decodes spells, or get a dragon to sit and heel? The only way to find out would be to go to Happilyeverafter and check it out in person.

6

# ANOTHER TIME...

That's why, with the help of the folks at the Gnomeplace Like Home Travel Agency, you have been booked on an exclusive, all-expenses-paid trip to the Land of Fairy Tales and Mother Goose. There, you'll discover the secrets of Snow White and the mysteries of Mother Hubbard's cupboard. You'll match wits with the Wise Men of Gotham, and test your speed against the Farmer's Wife (you know, the one with the carving knife). You'll even get the chance to meet, up-close and personal, mega-watt stars like Rapper Rapunzel and everyone's favorite bad boy, "B.B." Wolf.

So pack your bags with a sense of humor, and put your tongue in cheek. Then sit back and enjoy the trip of a lifetime. Just make sure you're back before midnight!

POOF

# Wanted: REWARD OFFERED!

The Sheriff of Nuttyham needs your help to track down these notorious felons! Please refer to the identification information on these pages, and look out for these criminals while visiting Happilyeverafter (a couple of them appear more than once).

## NAME: BIG BAD "B.B." WOLF

**DISTINGUISHING FEATURES:** big eyes, big ears—we already told you, he's big!

**LAST SEEN:** running away from Grandma's house

**WEARING:** nightgown, nightcap, fuzzy slippers

**ARMED WITH:** Very Big Teeth to eat you with; considered dangerous

**WANTED FOR:** identity theft

## NAME: THE WITCH

**DISTINGUISHING FEATURES:** sugary smile, always dressed in black

**LAST SEEN:** near the Gingerbread House at 252 Cookie Street

**WEARING:** black hat, black dress, black boots

**ARMED WITH:** gumdrops, spatula

**WANTED FOR:** baking and enter[tain]ing

8

**NAME: PUSS**

**DISTINGUISHING FEATURES:** furry ears and tail; makes odd purring sound

**LAST SEEN:** on the road to town

**WEARING:** tall boots, hat with feather

**ARMED WITH:** sword

**WANTED FOR:** fraud, extortion, and theft

**NAME: THE FARMER'S WIFE**

**DISTINGUISHING FEATURES:** evil glare in eye

**LAST SEEN:** in Fairy Tale Farmer's Market

**WEARING:** butchers' apron, rubber boots

**ARMED WITH:** a carving knife

**WANTED FOR:** assault with a deadly weapon

**NAME: THE TROLL**

**DISTINGUISHING FEATURES:** UG-LEE!

**LAST SEEN:** under a bridge

**WEARING:** evil grin

**ARMED WITH:** unrivaled riddle-solving abilities

**WANTED FOR:** obstruction, attempted "kid"napping

**NAME: JACK**

**DISTINGUISHING FEATURES:** bean-shaped birthmark, green thumb

HAIR

**LAST SEEN:** leaving the giant's castle in a hurry with a hen tucked under his arm

**WEARING:** running shoes; look for pockets bulging with beans

**ARMED WITH:** wits

**WANTED FOR:** grand larceny

**NAME: QUEEN JELOSIA**

**DISTINGUISHING FEATURES:** cackling laugh

**LAST SEEN:** in environs of the Magick Castle

**WEARING:** a cloak; may be disguised as an old woman

**ARMED WITH:** a poison apple

**WANTED FOR:** Administering an unlawful substance to a minor

158 for a list of locations where each of these felons was spotted in Happilyeveraft

## TRAVEL NOTES:

From within the storied halls of the **Magick Castle**, situated in the heart of Happilyeverafter, kings and queens have lorded it over the populace since once upon a time. Robust **knights** and glamorous **godmothers** mingle in the corridors, setting the latest fashions in hair, clothing, and party games for the whole kingdom.

Why just dream of the Magick Castle when you can experience it firsthand? The castle has recently been converted into a fabulous hotel by the hospitality chain Commonin Stay-a-Lot. During your stay, cheerful staff will pamper you with every **luxury**. Awake to a breakfast "fit for a king." Stroll in the enchanting (literally!) gardens or tour the royal estates in magnificent carriages complete with **mouse coachmen**.

At the end of the day, retire to your **royal chambers** and catch up on your beauty sleep in your own mile-high feather bed*.

*Premium surcharge for 100 years' sleep

**CURRENCY**
Gold, jewels, traveler's checks in very large denominations

**SUGGESTED LENGTH OF VISIT**
One Chapter

**DON'T MISS**
The Magick Castle's Great Tournament

# Kingly Calendar of Events

Hear Ye! Hear Ye! King Burpalot announces that the Great Tournament will be held at Magick Castle on Saturday, the Twelfth Day of the Month Taxemhard, and is now open to all contestants.

**Pumpkin Coach Racers**
Ride Closes at Midnight

**Burpalot Bumper Cars**
Now Gas-powered!

RIDES! RIDES! RIDES!

*The All New*
**Dragon WhipperSnapper Rollercoaster**

**Fairy-Go-Rounds and Fairess Wheels**
For the Littlest Imps

**Magic Mystery Mountain**

Run by Dwarf Mines Inc.

And more!

# Great Tournament Challenges
## Step Right Up and Test Your Skills

### CANDY-EATING CONTEST
Open to all boys and girls. Employees of the Gingerbread House Corp. prohibited. **Grand Prize**: A trip to Gluttonville!

### 5K FUN RUN
Open to Johnnycakes, Gingerbread Men, and Little Pigs. **Grand Prize**: Your very own brick dreamhouse!

### WIZARD SPELLING BEE
Witness the greatest wizards of our time spell off against one another in pursuit of the perfect potion.

### GOLD-SPINNING CONTESTS
Events in speed spinning, length of thread spun, and turning straw into gold.

### MOVE TO THE TRACKS
Laid down by **Rapper Rapunzel** and her crew, the Gift Wraps.

### PIE-BAKING CONTEST
All pies to be judged by Simple Simon. Win a blue ribbon for original creations! (Due to protests from animal rights groups, there will be no live-animal pies permitted in this year's event.)

### WILDEST HAIR CONTEST
Contestants to be judged on: longest hair, longest beard, and most hair growing from ears.

### WOOD-CUTTING TOURNAMENT
Prizes for fastest chopper, best team choppers, and best magical singing axe rendition of "The Lumberjack Song."

### BEANSTALK CLIMBING
**Grand Prize**: A hen that lays golden eggs.

### TEST YOUR STRENGTH
Arm-wrestle with Jack the Giant Killer. Only the strongest need apply. Large crowds expected so arrive early.

# Wizard Spelling Bee

*(oops!)*

The top wizards of Happilyeverafter have gathered for the annual spelling bee. You can help them by finding the spelling errors in each spell. Keep track of each wizard's mistakes on a piece of paper. The winning wizard is the one with the fewest errors. (Answers on page 158.)

## Wizard Walter of Wurmsen~Wurmsout

Take 15 onces of frog juce. Mix it with 6 noot eyes, 4 tongues of robbin, and precisely 13 french fries. Heat on a double-boiler untill mixture turns thick and bubbly. It should be a lovely shade of puce when dun.

Set to cool, then decant into a silver bottle. Use sparingly to turn victim into a toad.

## Wizard Mathilda of Meinz

To tern a prince's heart to stone, combine 6 drops of serpint drool with the perfuimed oils of the rare eglantine rose. Steep for twelve weeks. On midnihgt of the last day, chant, "Stone Heart, Stone Heart, from your princess you will part" over the vile. Slip the enchanted drool into the prince's morning oatmeal for instant rezults.

## Wizard Dragonbreath of Hoboken, New Jersey

Use this spell to make sure your clyent wins a televized wrestling match: "Fee, Fi, Fo, Fum, Certainly I'm not your chum, Too the mat I'll pin your tum, then win the cash—a princely sum!"

## Wizard Tiffany of Primadonna

This protecshun spell will prevent your enemies from enslaveing you into cleaning there ovens or washing their dirty socks. Take one eyelash, one nail cliping, and one skin flake. Combine with red jelly. Say "Shazam!" before eating. Repeat dayly for best results.

# KISS the FROG

Everyone knows that kissing a frog is supposed to turn it into a prince. While we won't guarantee that will happen when you play this really regal game, we can guarantee 100% fun!

## YOU'LL NEED

**large sheet of paper • markers**
**push pins or tape • scarf**
**3 or more players**
**pen/pencil and paper**

1 Draw a large picture of a frog on the sheet of paper. You can use the picture here as a model for your own crazy drawing. Color it in with the markers.

2 Assign point values to various parts of the frog's body. For example, anywhere on the legs is 5 points, the belly 10, the eyes 25, and the mouth, of course, 100 smackeroos.

3 Tape or pin the frog picture to a wall at eye level. (Make sure you get permission from an adult before you do this.)

4 Choose your first player. Using the scarf as a blindfold, tie it to cover the first player's eyes. No peeking!

5 Position the blindfolded player about 2 metres (6 feet) away from the frog picture. Make sure there are no obstacles between the player and the frog.

6 Count out, "1, 2, 3," as you turn the player around three times to mess up her sense of direction. Say "Go!" and release the player.

7 The blindfolded player must hold her hands behind her back and, by memory only, find her way to the picture. The object of the game is to get the most points by kissing the frog smack on the mouth.

8 Wherever the lips touch FIRST gives the player her score. The player can remove the blindfold and see for herself what part of the frog she's just smooched.

9 Keep track of each player's score with your pencil and paper. The winner is the player with the highest point score at the end.

25 points

5 points

5 points

100 points

10 points

5 points

5 points

**VARIATION** Cut out lip prints
in a different color for each player.
Roll up some tape behind each one.
Use these as the "kisses" to
stick on the frog.

17

# Frog FUNNIES

**(BECAUSE THERE ARE NEVER ENOUGH FROG JOKES)**

What's a frog's best year?

**A leap year!**

How does a frog feel when it has a broken leg?

**Unhoppy.**

What is a frog's favorite kind of music?

**Hip hop, of course.**

# WHAT DO YOU GET WHEN YOU CROSS A FROG WITH A...

...popsicle?

**Hopsicle**

...thief?

**A rob-it, rob-it**

...toaster?

Ribbit.

**Toadster**

...potato?

**Potatoad**

...genie's lamp?

**Rub-it, rub-it**

...pigeon?

**A pigeon-toed pigeon-toad**

19

# The Never-Ending

**T**ry this magical game the next time you and your friends are sitting around the castle hearth, digesting a roasted haunch of venison. It's also fun on car trips, when you're camping, and during sleepovers.

## YOU'LL NEED

**2 or more pals**

**1** The first player starts off the story with, "Once upon a time there was a...."

**2** The second player fills in the blank with anything they want to add. For example, "...six-toed, green-eyed, sloth-eating barracuda."

**3** The next player continues by adding a second sentence. "It was hungry for lunch—and was in the mood for flambéed fairy kebabs."

**4** The next player takes over, continuing the story by adding a sentence of his own. For example, "Meanwhile, Bobby J. Snodgrass was putting the finishing touches on his science project."

**5** Keep going like this, with each player adding sentence after sentence. In no time, you will wind up with one absolutely wild, kookier than kooky fairy tale!

**6** End your story with "And they all lived happily ever after" when you are laughing too hard to continue.

# Fairy Tale

## STORY STARTERS

Try some of these crazy sentences to get your never-ending fairy tale off to a wacky start.

Once upon a time there was ...

...an evil lawnmower.

...a giant with a bad case of dandruff.

...a village that was being terrorized by a dung beetle.

...a clown with a really bad attitude.

...a big bad wolf who never brushed his teeth.

...a fairy with thumbs as big as tractors.

...a talking pig, a talking goat, and a magic gym bag.

...a sock that smelled something funny.

...a giant lobster that was scared of its shadow.

...a wizard who wanted to create the world's best tuna sandwich.

...a girl named Prunella.

...a boy named Zitz.

...a prince, a pauper, and a pizza.

And so it came to pass that everything King Midas touched turned to **cold**.

# "THE QUEEN IS NOT AMUSED" PUZZLE

**J**oe the Jester played a mean trick on the Royal Family. At their annual dinner, he cast a spell on their name tags, so no one could find the correct seat.

The jester's secret code spell shifted each letter in the royal names by a few letters. Can you figure out the code and unscramble the names? If you do, you might get a Royal Pardon for the time you left the whoopee cushion on the queen's throne. Answers on page 158.

NRBBK MORKX

HFKD TFKDAFKD

Can I take your spot?

Move three spaces to the right, you say?

A B C D E

# Fairy Tale Whodunit

**T**he Royal Stepmother's Book of Spells has been stolen from the Crystal Room! Is the thief Sinister Cindy, Prince Conman, the (very bitter) Eighth Dwarf, or the Unfunny Jester?

At the time of the robbery, each one of the four suspects was in the castle. They were each wearing a different color outfit and carrying one of the four objects shown below.

WAND

PLATTER

LANCE

CROWN

The hidden cameras in the Crystal Room have caught a fuzzy picture of the thief.

## THE THRONE ROOM

Using the clues and picture below, figure out which object each suspect was carrying and what color each was wearing. You'll then know which fairy tale fiend did the dirty deed. Extra credit for figuring out where the other three suspects were at the time of the robbery. Solution on page 158.

**CLUE 1:**
The dwarf was not wearing blue, red, or yellow.

**CLUE 2:**
The person wearing green was not carrying a platter or lance.

**CLUE 3:**
Both the dwarf and the jester were holding an object that was made using a long stick.

**CLUE 4:**
The person with the platter of fish was not Cindy.

**CLUE 5:**
The person in red was delivering a platter of fish to a banquet.

THE GREAT HALL

THE KITCHEN

THE CRYSTAL ROOM

# Recipes *from the*

## Queen of Heart Tarts

### YOU'LL NEED

**1 roll of slice-and-bake biscuits**

**500 mL (2 cups) strawberries, washed and sliced**

**30 mL (2 tablespoons) sugar, or to taste**

**canned whipped cream**

**mint leaves (optional)**

### YOU'LL ALSO NEED

**baking sheet • measuring spoons**
**knife • mixing bowl • mixing spoon**

1. Have an adult help you to prepare the biscuits according to the package directions. Let cool, about 15 minutes.

2. While the biscuits are cooling, place the sliced berries in a mixing bowl. Sprinkle the sugar over the berries. Stir with the mixing spoon.

3. For each guest, cut one biscuit crosswise in half. Place both halves on a serving plate.

4. Squirt a generous serving of whipped cream on both halves of the biscuit. Then spoon the strawberry and sugar mixture over the whipped cream.

5. Add another squirt of whipped cream and a mint leaf to garnish, if desired.

**Yield:** the number of biscuits in your package
**Prep time:** 30 minutes

# Castle Kitchens

## All the King's Grilled Cheese Soldiers

1. Lay two slices of bread on your work surface.

2. Lay one slice of cheese on each piece of bread.

3. Top each slice of cheese with the remaining slices of bread.

4. Using the cookie cutter, cut out a "soldier" from each sandwich. If you start at one side of the sandwich, you may be able to cut out two complete soldiers from each one.

5. Using the knife, spread the top of each solider sandwich with a coating of margarine or butter. Carefully turn the soldier over and butter the other side.

6. Get an adult to help you with this step. Turn the stove element on to medium high. Using the spatula, place each soldier into the frying pan.

7. Fry until the underside is golden brown, two to three minutes.

8. When the bottom of the soldier is cooked, carefully flip it over with the spatula. Continue cooking until the cheese is melted and the second side is brown, about one minute.

9. Serve and eat!

**Yield:** serves 2 • **Prep time:** 10 minutes

### YOU'LL NEED
**4 slices bread**
**2 slices cheddar cheese**
**margarine or butter**

### YOU'LL ALSO NEED
**gingerbread man cookie cutter**
**knife • frying pan**
**spatula**

29

# Castle SCAVENGER HUNT

**A** golden goose has been hidden somewhere in Happilyeverafter. To find it you will have to go on a wild goose chase of your own— through the pages of this book. Here's what to do: Read the clues below in order. Each one will send you to another page in this book. From there, follow the clues that will send you to yet another page. And so on, and so on, until at last, if you are clever enough to solve all the riddles, you will find the hidden fowl. Are you up to the challenge? Then get quacking with Goose Clue number 1.

**1**
Once upon a time
(Tickety-tock),
Start your hunt on
The first page with
a clock.

**2**
From the clock
Turn a few pages more,
Find a sad princess
With hair to the floor.

**3**
Do you also see
A horse and carriage there?
Gallop forward seven pages,
If you dare!

**4**
Here's a frog
With a number on his tum.
It's that number of pages ahead
Smart frogs should
hop or run.

**5**
The castle kitchen is
A clue for you
To find the page with a recipe
For peas porridge stew.

**6**
Pease porridge hot,
Pease porridge cold,
Go forward four more pages
Before the trail gets old.

**7**
Wise men you'll find a-floating
On the soupy sea
Turn two dozen pages
back from there,
Can you find piggies three?

**8**
Go back the number of pages
For each piggy that you see.
It won't be one or even two
You'll have to turn
back three.

**10**
What does Jack need
to complete his home?
Elephants dancing in threes,
not alone.
Skip to the page
(and help save the day)
Where you find elephants
doing ballet.

**9**
Eek! It's a mouse!
Run forward fifteen
All the way to
Jack's house.

**11**
The number of tutus
Plus one tutu more
Gives you the "two + two"
Number of four.

**12**
Turn back
these four pages
And climb up the vine
That magical goose
Is finally thine!

Answers on page 158.

# EXTRA! EXTRA!

# Prince Valiant Shares His "How to Be a Hero" Secrets!

**P.U.: Prince Valiant, how did you ever get so handsome (*giggle*)?**

**Prince:** Aw, shucks. I just try to stay in good health by wrestling a few trolls before breakfast.

**P.U.: We were all riveted by the story of how you saved Princess Vitamina from the Gnomes of Ullaska. Tell us what happened.**

**Prince:** It was nothing, really. I heard that Vita—

that's what I call her—had gotten herself into a peck of trouble. The gnomes have very strict rules about chewing gum in their realm. Well, Vita has a thing for blowing super-gigantic bubbles. She's trying to make it into the Fairyland Book of Records for world's biggest bubble. Anyway, she blew this big bubble and it popped really loudly, right outside the gnome king's guard room. Vita was beat!

**P.U.: So what did you do?**

**Prince:** I leapt onto my noble steed and dashed

# EXCLUSIVE NEWSPAPER INTERVIEW

**Prince Valiant, one of Happilyeverafter's most notable celebs, has agreed to share a little of his private life with the _Herald_. Here is the interview that I, Penelope Ubsequiessa, conducted with him in his royal suites.**

off to Ullaska, of course. Got there just in time. Apparently Vita was being tortured by being made to blow double bubbles without cease.

I made quite a heroic entrance, if I do say so myself. I swept up the princess and we rode out of the dungeons to safety.

**P.U.: That's an inspiring tale. Is there anything between you and Princess Vitamina of a (_giggle_) more romantic nature?**

**Prince:** Vita? No. She's just a great pal. Last I heard she's involved with that Charming dude.

**P.U.: So who's the lucky gal? Snow White? Rapunzel? There were stories in the press linking you to both of those lovely ladies last year.**

**Prince:** Well, you may know that I had a thing with Snow for a while. Seemed she was living with some evil dwarves who cooked up a plot to enslave her. My mother acted as a spy and got her out of there by giving her an apple with a powerful sedative in it. She woke up later on and was so relieved to find me hovering over her that she kissed me right on the lips. I was bowled

over, let me tell you. She's quite a gal.

**P.U.: What about Rapunzel?**

**Prince:** She was having some family troubles. I helped bust her out of her tower, that's true. But Rapi has other plans. She's thinking politics, once she's had a run at a musical career.

**P.U.: So what advice would you give to youngsters who want to be a hero like you?**

**Prince:** Always eat breakfast. It's the most important meal of the day!

# FREE
## ~~Princess Vitamina!~~
### Prince Valiant!

There are two sides to every story. According to late-breaking news from Princess Vitamina's press secretary, it was actually an embarrassed Prince Valiant who had gotten himself in a jam and needed a helping hand from the princess. The princess discovered that Prince Valiant was being held in a dungeon cell by the Gnomes of Ullaska. The dungeon was filled with keys, but which one opened his cell?

Vitamina discovered that when a key is inserted into the lock, a numbered coin pops out the other side. The coin can then be put into the door's coin slot. If the correct coin were inserted into the slot, Prince Valiant would be freed.

Vitamina had been given three chances to guess the correct key. After her second attempt, a good fairy helped her out by giving her a big clue. The fairy said that only a 25-cent coin will open the dungeon door.

This made her task much easier, but Vitamina still had to figure out which key to choose to get the 25-piece coin. Only one key would work!

Look at the dungeon log book below. It shows Prince Valiant's mother's three guesses (she failed to free her sonny bunny) and Princess Vitamina's first two guesses.

Can you figure out which key Princess Vitamina used to rescue the prince? **HINT:** the princess used her math skills to think about the relationship between the number on the key and the number on the coin. Answer on page 158.

| ATTEMPTING RESCUER | KEY | COIN | RESULT |
|---|---|---|---|
| Prince's Mommy | 5 | 16 | Failed |
| Prince's Mommy | 3 | 10 | Failed |
| Prince's Mommy | 2 | 7 | Failed – Mrs. Valiant sent to remedial math classes with Old Woman Who Lived in a Shoe |
| Vita | 1 | 4 | Failed |
| Vita | 10 | 31 | Failed |
| Vita | ? | 25 | Ding! Ding! Ding! |

# Royal RIDDLES

What do you call blackbirds in a pastry dish?

Tweetie Pie!

Why did Cinderella get kicked off the baseball team?

She was always running away from the ball!

Why was Cinderella such a lousy baseball player?

She had a pumpkin for a coach.

What does an evil witch like to read in the newspaper?

Her horror scope.

Why do dragons sleep all day?

So they can fight knights.

What's gray, has a wand, and gives money to elephants?

**The tusk fairy!**

Why were the giant's fingers only eleven inches long?

**Because if they were twelve inches long, they'd be a foot!**

Why did the Fairy Stepmother cross the road?

**The chicken was temporarily unavailable as it had been turned into a pumpkin.**

What's Snow White's brother's name?

**Egg White! Get the yolk?**

What do frog princes like to eat with their hamburgers?

**French flies.**

What did the princess say when her photographs weren't ready?

**Some day my prints will come!**

Why was Snow White elected judge?

**She was the fairest in the land.**

# Cinderella,

You know how the famous story says that Cinderella jumped into the pumpkin coach to go to the ball? Well, according to storytellers the world over, Cinderella didn't stop at the palace. This world traveler kept on going. In fact, she hit every major continent— and sent the postcards home to prove it!

**80分**
**CHINA**

Dear Fairy Godmom,

Having an OK time here in China. I've been living with a crabby old lady who killed my only friend, a magic fish. Luckily, an old man told me to gather up the fish bones and use them to make a wish. I did, and guess what? I wished for a chance to go the Spring Festival (my guide book says it's "worth a look"), and poof! A gorgeous outfit and the sweetest pair of gold shoes appeared. Can't wait to wear them!

I'll write again with the report about the festival after I go.

Take care, love ya,
"Yeh-Shen" (it's me, Cindy)

# World Traveler

Dear Snow W,

I met this fantastic black hen who can whip up clothes like nobody's business. Today I'm wearing what she made for me: A dress as red as a rose from the waist down and as white as, well, you, from the waist up. It has a matching green cape, a hat with red, white, and green feathers, and shoes with the toes red, the middles white, and the backs and heels green. I'm supposed to be meeting this cute prince today!

Wish me luck!
Cindy (in Ireland!)

€1
IRELAND

## Ireland

Variations of the Cinderella story can be found in the folk legends of virtually every country in the world. She goes by "Yeh-Shen" in **China**, "Rashin-Coatie" in **Scotland**, "Katie Woodencloak" in **Norway**, "The Rough-Face Girl" in **North American Native** legend, "Chinye" and "Nyasha" in **Africa**, "Tattercoats" in **England**, "Pepelyouga" in **Serbia**, "Aschenputtel" in **Germany**, and "Liisa" in **Finland**. Scholars think there may actually be as many as 3,000 different versions of the Cinderella story!

## Cinderella Story Checklist

• kind but picked-on girl at the mercy of a step-family

• neglectful or absent dad

• magical guardian

• an ending in which the girl winds up with the prize and her persecutors get "payback"

## Which Cindy Do You Prefer?

In many modern versions of the Cinderella story, Cinderella is portrayed as beautiful and helpless, more like a doll than a real woman. In most of the traditional stories, however, Cinderella succeeds thanks to her cleverness and goodness.

Dear Rapunzel,

I'm in West Africa! I met an old lady who told me to go into this run-down hut and get a tiny gourd. (Something about me and pumpkins, huh?) Anyway, I did, and when I got home (I'm boarding with a family and have two African "sisters") I cracked open the gourd and treasure spilled out. Was my stepsister ticked! She ran out and, without even asking for permission, took the biggest gourd in the hut (she's pretty greedy). When she cracked hers open, there was no treasure, but a wicked storm started—blew me right out of town! Don't know where I'm headed next.

Will keep you posted. How's the hair growing?

With love,
"Chinye" (Cindy in West Africa)

Dear Sleeping Beauty,

This will wake you up! Guess what happened to me here in Canada: I got lost in the woods, and two sisters took me in. At first they were nice, but then they started to treat me like their slave. They made me tend the fire for hours. I got sleepy and got too close—sparks flew up and now I've got these horrid marks on my face!!! Anyway, I keep seeing this guy that no one else can. He's supposed to be a magic chieftain. I'm putting on my best birchbark dress and going to see if he can help me out.

Love ya, write soon,
Rough-Face (ha-ha, it's just me, Cindy)

Dear Sleeping B,

HOT UPDATE: The guy was a magic chieftain after all! He showed me how to get rid of the burns on my face by bathing in a magic lake. He wanted to marry me, but I figure I've had enough of this part of the world for now. I'm heading out tomorrow—who knows where? I'll write when I get. . .wherever!

Love,
Cindy

Ontario

# Dragon CATCHER

If you want to spend time with fairy tale royalty you'd better be ready to talk about dragons. Now you can tell your own tales of capturing one of the fire-breathing beasts!

## YOU'LL NEED

pencil or pen

tracing paper

scissors

one blank 3 x 5 inch index card, cut in half vertically

crayons or markers

clear tape

TRACE

46

1. Draw a cage on one of the index card halves, or copy the picture from the opposite page onto tracing paper and transfer it to one of the index card halves. Color.

2. Trace the dragon picture and transfer the drawing in the same way as you did with the cage to the other index card half (or just draw your own dragon onto the index card).

3. Place the cage picture face down on the table.

4. Lay your pencil on the index card. The pencil tip should point up, roughly in line with the top edge of the card. Use a piece of tape to fasten the pencil into place.

5. Pull off two more pieces of tape, each about 2.5 cm (1 in.) long, from the roll. Twist them each into a loop. Stick the loops onto the card, one on either side of the pencil.

6. Lay the dragon picture, face-up, on top of the pencil and tape loops. Squish flat so the "sandwich" is stuck together.

7. Your dragon-catcher is done. To put it into action, hold the pencil upright between your two palms. Rub the pencil quickly back and forth between your hands so it spins.

8. Can you see the dragon being captured in the cage? Congratulations! You are a real dragon catcher!

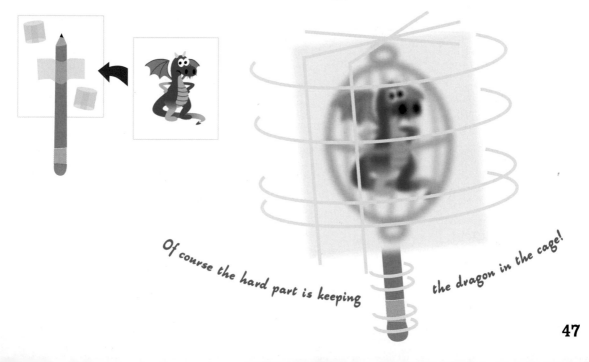

Of course the hard part is keeping the dragon in the cage!

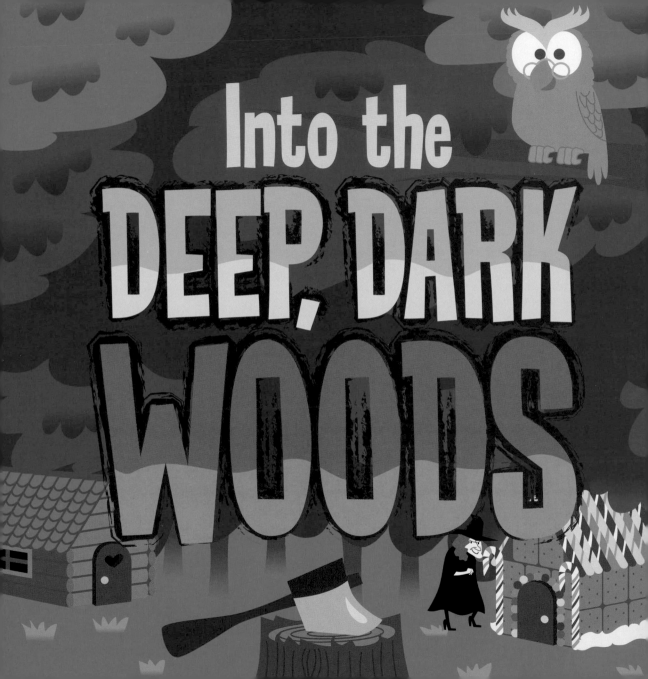

# Into the
# DEEP, DARK
# WOODS

## TRAVEL NOTES:

Fairy Tale Forest hosts a wide variety of **wildlife** including bears (in three sizes), wolves, and trolls. A thriving community of **fairies** lives deep in its glades; travelers should remain alert to these mischievous creatures. Intrepid visitors may catch a rare glimpse of *Lizardia halitosis*. This endangered animal, a.k.a the Fire-Breathing Dragon, has been a protected species since 1066.

The **forest dwellers** are an enterprising people who engage in many trades including woodcutting, pencil engineering, and spell decoding. They can be heard bursting into renditions of that forest favorite, "Hi Ho, Hi Ho!"

Well-marked **hiking trails** will take you past Sure Wood, and the Village of the Seven Dwarves. Scenic highlights include Sleeping Beauty's Castle at the forest edge (now a National Heritage Site and Sleep Disorder Clinic), the Fairy Kingdom (you will need your passport to visit), and the Dragon's Lair (enter only with a guide).

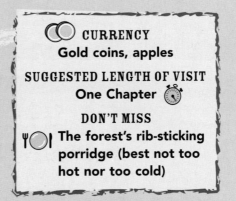

**CURRENCY**
Gold coins, apples

**SUGGESTED LENGTH OF VISIT**
One Chapter

**DON'T MISS**
The forest's rib-sticking porridge (best not too hot nor too cold)

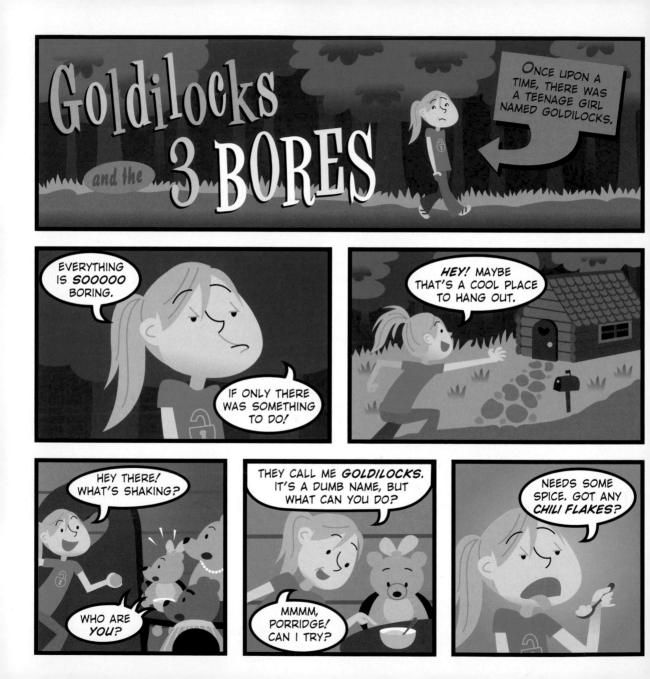

# Lost in the Woods...

Start Here

cliff

■NOW WHIT■'S HOME

WI■E OLD O■L'S TREE

HAN■EL & GR■TEL'S HOME

Dragon's Lair

B■A■T'S LAIR

■OLF'S CRO■SING

HU■TER'S D■ELLING

OLD CRO■'S N■ST PASS

Troll Town · DO NOT ENTER

52

Can you find your way through the Fairy Tale Forest? Enter at the arrow. At each landmark, there is a sign that is missing two letters. The missing letters stand for directions: N for north, S for south, E for east, and W for west. Figure out what letters are missing, then choose which direction of the two you want to go (only one is right!). Continue until you arrive safely at the Jolly Miller's Inn, or take a wrong turn and end up in the Dragon's Lair. Check your path on page 158. Good luck!

END

WITCH HAZEL HOLLOW

Jolly Miller's Inn

DWARF TOWN

N

W

E

S

# Hear Ye! Hear Ye! Step Right

Trolls love to hide in the forest—especially under bridges. Don't be alarmed if you find one blocking your path. They will let you pass if you challenge them to solve a riddle. They love riddles! But it's got to be a good one. Try your hand at these classic riddles. The one at the right has been solved for you. (Answers on page 159.)

I go through the mud
And through the mud
I only leave one track.

**What am I?**

# Up and Stump the Troll!

Little Nancy Etticoat
With a white petticoat
And a red nose;
She has no feet nor hands
And the longer she stands
The shorter she grows!

In spring I sashay
Decked in fancy array
In summer more clothing I wear;
When colder it grows
I fling off my clothes!
And in winter go totally bare.

**What is Nancy Etticoat?**

**What am I?**

**ANSWER:** A tree.

# Goofiness in the Fairy Tale Forest

**I**n this hilarious game, two teams compete to see whose wolf can be the first to disguise himself as Little Red Riding Hood's granny.

## YOU'LL NEED

**2 or more kids**

**2 EACH:**

chairs • large pairs of pants • large shirts • pairs of socks • pairs of shoes
pairs of gloves • suspenders • scarves • knit caps • long flannel nightgowns
pairs of bedroom slippers • floppy hats • pairs of pantyhose • whistles

*Peeeet!*

# Big Bad Wolf Race

1 Each team chooses one player to be the wolf.

2 To start, each wolf puts the following "wolf" clothing items on, on top of his or her everyday clothes: a large pair of pants, a large shirt, socks, a pair of shoes, gloves, suspenders, a scarf, and a knit cap.

3 At "Go!" each wolf must remove his or her wolf clothing as quickly as possible. The wolf must then put on Granny's clothes from a pile nearby: pantyhose, a long flannel nightgown, bedroom slippers, and a floppy hat.

4 As soon as the wolf is dressed completely as Granny, he or she must run to the chair, sit down, and blow the whistle. The first wolf to blow the whistle is the winner.

5 Play as many times as there are wolves who want to compete!

# Fairy Lore—and More!

The fairy tale forest is home to lots of fairies. Don't be fooled by their delicate appearance. Fairies pack a wallop when it comes to magic, and they can be downright tricky.

Come across a bunch of fairies **dancing in a glen,** and you might want to join in. The problem is, fairy magic won't let you stop! You'll bop 'til you drop.

**Mind your p's and q's** with fairies. One wrong word and these unpredictable critters may trap you in a tree for eternity.

Fairies are not all bad. They'll help you in a pinch if you are kind and generous. They love **well-mannered kids.**

## A Fairly Scary Fairy Story

Finding a **four-leaf clover** is considered lucky, but do you know why? It's believed you can use one to break fairy spells.

**A daisy chain** may protect you from fairy mischief! Collect about a dozen daisies with long stems. Use your fingernail to make a slit in the stem of a daisy. Slip the stalk of a second flower through the slit. Repeat until all twelve daisies are chained together. Tie the first and last daisies together into a loop. Wear as a necklace or on your head like a crown.

WIPE WIPE WIPE

# Dear Fairy

## "Good Advice from a Very Good Fairy!"

Dear F.G.,

Can you help me? I am being evilly used by my family. They make me do all of the housework and never let me go out to have any fun. My sisters tease me all the time. I think this is because they are jealous of me—they are not exactly easy on the eyes. Last week, I heard that there's going to be this fab party up at the castle. All the girls in town are invited, but my stepmom won't let me go.

What should I do?

Signed,
Sad, Sad Cindy

Dear Sad, Sad,

Would you believe me if I said your luck was about to change? Things will become different around your house, big time.

Forget about your stepmom and rotten sisters. I know it's not easy, but you are so close to moving on out and up. Just hang in there a few more days.

Plan on going to that ball, and get busy sewing up a dress. I'm sure you'll be able to find some pals to help you. And if you have a chance to get a pedicure, go for it.

Have fun at the party!

F.G.

Can you identify the well-known character and story that each letter writer is from? Answers on page 15

# Godmother

Dear F.G,

I have been suffering from an irrational fear my whole life. My two brothers keep telling me I have nothing to worry about, but every time I hear the word "wolf" I break out into a cold sweat. What should I do?

Yours,
Little Pig

Dear Little Pig,

Being wary of wolves is not irrational. It shows that you understand that life can be dangerous, that you can't trust everyone you meet, and that you need to take precautions. I suggest you buy yourself some nice sturdy bricks and build a solid little house that will make you feel safe and secure.

F.G.

63

Dear F.G.,

I am soooo mad at my father! I am a vegetarian, but he keeps ordering totally gross foods to be served for dinner. Last night—if you can believe this—he served blackbirds baked in a pie! LIVE!!!! I wanted to barf.

Help!
Disgusted

Dear F.G.,

I am writing to you because I am at the end of my shoelace. I live in a very small house and I have so many children. I don't know what to do! Last night, I was so frustrated, I gave them some broth without any bread, whipped them all soundly, and sent them to bed. I know this was the wrong thing to do, but I simply can't cope.

Feeling Like a Heel

**Dear Disgusted,**

**Perhaps he will respect your wishes if you express them in a mature way. You might also try bringing home some vegetarian dishes for him to try. I suggest pies from the Pieman. They are often made with plums and are very delicious.**

**F.G.**

**Dear Heel,**

**Recognizing that you have a problem is the first step towards solving it. You do need help, and fast! May I suggest you contact Old Mother Hubbard? She has lots of space in her house (she shares it with only a little dog), and could use some work. I think if you teamed up, you'd both be much better off.**

**F.G.**

Dear F.G.,

I accidentally swallowed a fly last night. It keeps buzzing around inside me. I'm thinking that perhaps I should swallow a spider to swallow that fly, but I'm not sure if I should. Please advise.

Rumbly in My Tumbly

**Dear Rumbly,**

By no means should you compound your problem by swallowing a spider! That would start you down a slippery slope. The next thing you know, you'll be swallowing birds, cats, dogs, horses, you name it. And none of that will do a darn bit of good for that fly.

I suggest you visit Miss Spider for tea. Once you are at her place, she may be able to entice the fly into her parlor. Then you will be free of your buzzing pest.

F.G.

# WRITE YOUR OWN

# FAIRY TALE

You can complete this magically incomplete fairy tale! Write the numbers 1 to 26 on a piece of paper. Read out the list at the right, recording your friend's answers beside the numbered list. Then read out the fairy story on the next page, filling in the words that your friend supplied for each number.

## YOU'LL NEED
**a friend**
paper
**pencil or pen**

**Write down the words your friend supplies according to this list:**

1 an adjective (a word that describes something, e.g. gorgeous, funny, odd, purple)
2 a kind of feeling (scared, lonely, excited)
3 a piece of clothing
4 a thing
5 another thing
6 a verb (an action word), past tense (e.g. kissed, danced, exploded)
7 a kind of animal
8 a kind of person (e.g. sailor, teacher, carpenter)
9 a verb, present tense (e.g. sing, play, climb)
10 something your teacher says when she is annoyed
11 another verb, past tense
12 another adjective
13 funny things
14 more funny things
15 a verb with a sound (e.g. buzzed, hooted, screeched)
16 a kind of animal
17 an unusual thing
18 a thing
19 a weird animal
20 another verb, past tense
21 an icky thing
22 a silly thing
23 a kind of food
24 another adjective
25 another verb, present tense
26 another verb, past tense

nce upon a time there was a **(1)** princess. She was very **(2)** all alone in her castle. So she decided to go on an adventure. She donned a **(3)**, a **(4)**, and a **(5)**, **(6)** her mother goodbye and set off on her noble **(7)**.

Before long she came to a bridge. Beneath it, there was an ugly **(8)** who said, "Answer this riddle or I will **(9)** with you."

The princess said, "**(10)**!" Then she **(11)** the **(8)** and continued on her way.

A little while later the princess came to a **(12)** forest. It was full of **(13)** and **(14)**. The owls **(15)**.

A little old **(16)** came up to her and said, "Where are you going?"

She replied, "To find my **(17)**."

The little old **(16)** said, "Take this **(18)**. When you meet a **(19)** on the road, **(20)** it at it. It will turn into a **(21)**.

The princess thanked the old **(16)** and continued into the dark forest.

It was not long before a **(19)** blocked her way. She **(20)** her **(18)** at the **(19)** and it turned into a **(21)**.

The princess put the **(21)** in her pocket. She began to feel strange. All the trees turned into **(22)** and the sky was the color of **(23)**!

The princess screamed and threw the **(21)** away.

When the **(21)** bounced on the road it turned into a **(24)** prince. The prince swept the princess up on his arms. He said, "You have broken my enchantment! Now I will **(25)** you and we will live happily ever after."

The princess **(26)** and said, "No way am I going to **(25)** a **(19)**. She got back on her **(7)** and disappeared into the deep, dark woods. And she was never seen in Fairyland again.

# JOKES

## From the Fairytale Forest

Who did the fish tell his wish to?

His fairy cod mother.

What did the dragon say when it saw a knight in armor?

Oh, no! Not more canned food!

Why did the fairy princess go to the dentist?

To get her teeth crowned.

Knock, knock.

Who's there?

Dragon.

Dragon who?

Just me, dragon my feet again!

Why did the boy refuse to board the boat?

He said he didn't believe in ferries.

What stories do the ship captain's children like to hear?

Ferry tales!

What forest dweller is always hungry?

A goblin.

What's the difference between a pixie's desire for wings and a doubtful trout?

One's a fairy's wish and the other's a wary fish.

What do witches put on their hair?

Scare gel.

Why is the tooth fairy so smart?

She's collected lots of wisdom teeth.

Where do you go to learn how to fight dragons?

Knight school!

What do you call a fairy who won't take a bath?

Stinkerbell.

How do you send a message in the fairy forest?

By moss code.

Knock, knock. Who's there? Fairy. Fairy who? Fairy nice to meet you.

**69**

# TOOTH FAIRY TRIVIA

She's the fairy we all know best. Or, at least we think we do! Sink your teeth into these little known facts about the thief of teeth (say *that* five times fast).

In ancient times, people believed that teeth held powerful magic! They believed they could be used to **ward off witches and demons**. On the other hand, if a witch were to get a hold of someone's tooth, she could use it to gain control over them.

The **Vikings** were so desperate to use baby teeth as charms that these fearless warriors begged their kids for them. Clever Viking tots held out for cold, hard cash, becoming the first kids in recorded history to turn their molars into moolah.

The **Ancient Egyptians** threw their baby teeth to the sun. They believed the sun would provide them with strong teeth.

In **Botswana**, children threw their baby teeth over the roof, chanting, "Mr. Moon, Mr. Moon, Please bring me a new tooth." Invariably, the moon did just that!

If you're in Spain, expect your tooth-taker not to be a fairy but a mouse! The midnight mouseketeer, **Ratoncito Perez**, is so popular in Spain that the mayor of Madrid placed a commemorative plaque on the home where Ratoncito once lived.

Noted toothfairyologist Rosemary Wells tracked the **exchange rate** for teeth (how much money a lost tooth earned from the tooth fairy) from 1900 to 1980. She found that the tooth fairy pay scale kept up with inflation!

# WHAT JAMES OLIVER QUACKENBUSH FOUND UNDER HIS PILLOW:

Dear [insert child's name here]. James,

Thank you for leaving [ 1 ] tooth/teeth under your pillow. While we make every attempt to leave a monetary reward, we were unable to process yours for the following reason(s):

( ) the tooth could not be found
(X) it was not a human tooth
( ) tooth rejected due to excessive fairy-repellent plaque
( ) the tooth has already been redeemed for cash— double-dipping is expressly prohibited
(X) the tooth did not originally belong to you
( ) the tooth fairy won't process tooth-shaped cheese rinds
(X) you were overheard to state that you do not believe in the tooth fairy
( ) you were age 12 or older at the time of your request
( ) the tooth is still in your mouth
( ) the tooth was guarded by a vicious fairy-eating dog at the time of our visit (see Tooth Fairy Guidelines re. Dealing with Birds, Rodents, Canines, and Dustmites)

Sincerely,

T. F.

The Tooth Fairy

Drat.

# Fairy Wand ZSPEFLL DECODER

Fairies keep their spells secret by writing them in a mysterious fairy rune language. But you have found a fairy wand that really works! If you wave it over the spell, it turns the writing into English that you can read!

## YOU'LL NEED

tracing paper

pencil

scissors

cardboard

markers or crayons

20 x 30 cm (8 in. x 12 in.) sheet of red cellophane (available from an art or office/school supplies store)

tape

## Follow these directions to decode the fairy spells written on these rocks (right).

1. Trace the outline of the fairy wand (at right). Cut out the shape in the tracing paper, then copy the outline of the design onto your cardboard.

2. Cut out the wand. Use your markers or crayons to color as desired.

3. Cut out the rectangular "window" in the wand's stem. Then cut out a larger rectangle of red cellophane from the sheet to cover the window.

4. Cover the back of the window in your wand with the cellophane. Tape the cellophane in place.

Wave your wand so that the red "window" slides over the rocks below. You should be able to read the secret spells!

TRACE

I'llsdancerwithingyourtcircled
sandybringtyoursheart'sodeblight
stiffyou'lllmakermentheyvictory
koftmynnexterbigspillowmfight.

Arthimbledfullcofsmilkweedajuice
lnofferttowyournow
inghopeshyouswillonotscomettonight
topstealnourtpurplekcow.

Starlight,astarbright
firsthstartlfseentonight
lnwishalrmayolnwishelfmight
ongmyespellingotest,egets"principal"fright.

# Recipes from the

Hiking through the Fairy Tale Forest sure helps you work up an appetite. Here's what to eat on your journey.

## Three Bears Porridge

**This recipe makes oatmeal that's not too hot, not too cold, not too sweet, and not too runny. It's more than "just right"—it's perfect!**

### YOU'LL NEED

750 mL (3 cups) water
2.5 mL (1/2 teaspoon) salt
325 mL (1 1/3 cups) quick cooking oats
60 mL (1/4 cup) raisins (optional)
pinch of ground cinnamon
60 mL (4 tablespoons) brown sugar
60 mL (1/4 cup) milk (optional)

### YOU'LL ALSO NEED

measuring cup • measuring spoons
medium-sized saucepan with lid
mixing spoon • bowls and spoons

1. Ask an adult to help you with steps 1 to 4. In the saucepan, combine water and salt. Cover and bring to a boil.

2. Remove lid and reduce heat to low. Add oats. Add raisins, if using. Stir.

3. Allow the oatmeal to cook, covered, for about five minutes or until thickened. Stir occasionally.

4. When the oatmeal has reached the desired consistency, remove from heat.

5. Add cinnamon and brown sugar. Mix well. Serve in bowls, with milk poured over top if desired.

6. Any uneaten oatmeal can be stored in the fridge and reheated in the microwave to eat later.

**Yield:** 4 portions • **Prep time:** 15 minutes

## "Poison" Apples

**Snow White couldn't resist when she was offered these tempting treats. You won't be able to resist them either.**

### YOU'LL NEED

250 gram (8 ounce) package light cream cheese (let it warm up to room temperature so it gets soft)

175 mL (3/4 cup) brown sugar

250 mL (1 cup) light sour cream

10 mL (2 teaspoons) vanilla

10 mL (2 teaspoons) lemon juice

250 mL (1 cup) milk (1% or skim)

1 package (113 grams/4 ounce) vanilla instant pudding mix

6 apples, cored and sliced (an adult should help you do this)

### YOU'LL ALSO NEED

measuring cup • measuring spoons mixing bowl • mixing spoon

1. Combine the cream cheese and brown sugar in the mixing bowl.

2. Add the rest of the ingredients (except apples) one at a time, mixing well after each addition.

3. Chill in the fridge until cold, about an hour.

4. When it is cold, serve with the sliced apples for dipping. Remember to cackle wickedly as you offer the plate around.

**Yield:** 48 apple slices, enough for 1 fairy tale princess or 6 real life kids

**Prep time:** 15 minutes

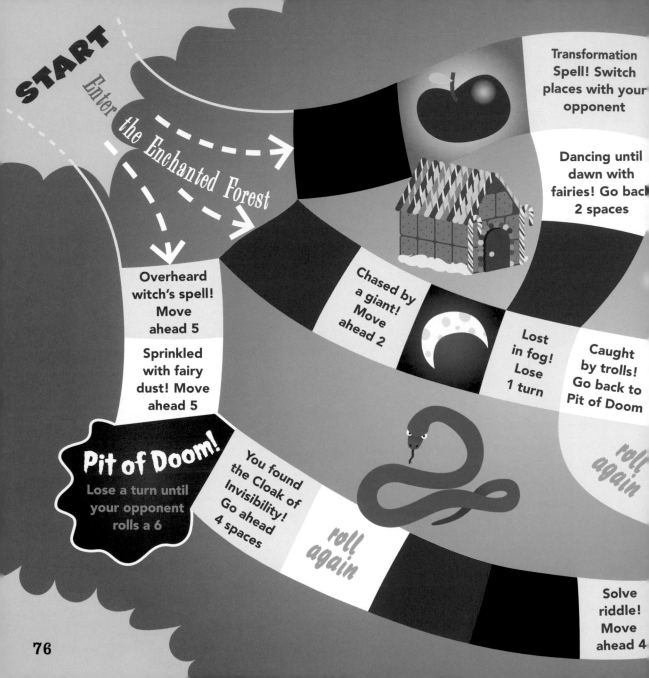

START

Enter the Enchanted Forest

Transformation Spell! Switch places with your opponent

Dancing until dawn with fairies! Go back 2 spaces

Overheard witch's spell! Move ahead 5

Chased by a giant! Move ahead 2

Lost in fog! Lose 1 turn

Caught by trolls! Go back to Pit of Doom

Sprinkled with fairy dust! Move ahead 5

roll again

Pit of Doom!
Lose a turn until your opponent rolls a 6

You found the Cloak of Invisibility! Go ahead 4 spaces

roll again

Solve riddle! Move ahead 4

# Race through the Enchanted Forest

## board game

**Pricked your finger! Fall asleep for 1 turn**

**Meet Beast He's a prince! Move ahead 2**

**Storm! Go back 1**

**Discover Golden Goose! Go ahead 1**

**Go Back to Start!**

### YOU'LL NEED

**a friend • 2 different coins or buttons to use as your markers • a die**

The player with the curliest hair goes first by moving the number of spaces rolled on the die. In this game you can choose different paths. Choose carefully—the shortest path might not be the safest! The first player to make it through the forest wins.

*You're Safe! Free as a bird!*

# HERE BE DRAGONS

**N**o self-respecting fairy tale forest could be without its own Dragon-in-Residence. Best to find out as much as you can about these beasts before you enter.

**Dragon Boa Racing** originated ir China over 2,00( years ago. According to tradition, the great Heavenly Dragon, ruler of the seas and rivers and bringer of clouds and rain, hibernated during the winter. The dragon boat festival each spring would awaken the dragon and ensure a good summer crop.

The word "dragon" comes from the **Greek word drakōn**, meaning "that which sees" or "that which flashes." It may have originally referred to a type of snake with shiny scales.

The **oldest** written account of dragons is in the ancient epic *Gilgamesh*, a Sumerian story from about 3000 B.C.

In China, dragons are emblems of **royalty**, but in traditional European stories, dragons are often symbols of **greed**.

**Viking ships** used dragon figureheads at the front to scare off sea monsters.

To figure out where an Eastern dragon comes from, check out its toes. If it has **five claws** on each foot, it most likely comes from China; **three claws**, Japan; and **four claws**, Korea. What gives? The Chinese say that dragons originated in China, and *lose* toes as they emigrate further from their homeland. The Japanese have a different idea. They say that dragons originated in Japan and *grew* toes as they traveled.

**Marco Polo**, upon visiting China, reported that the royal chariot was pulled by dragons. And we all know that Marco Polo *never* exaggerated. Not one bit!

As late as 1611, the **Chinese emperor** had his very own "Royal Dragon Feeder" (hope this post was for feeding the dragons, not being fed *to* the dragons!).

The **Thai Dragon** may not actually breathe fire but it sure is hot. The term refers to an Asian chili pepper that is 20 times hotter than a jalapeno!

# MORE DRAGON LORE

The **national flag of Wales** shows a red dragon on a green and white field. The dragon has been used as a symbol of Wales since at least 820 A.D.

Another common name for Western dragons is wyrm, or **"worm."** This name usually refers to snaky, water-dwelling dragons, but can be used for any dragon. Wyrms were thought to be especially common in Britain. The best-known is Nessie, Scotland's Loch Ness Monster.

An **ancient British legend** describes how King Vortigern was trying to build a temple on Salisbury Plain. When it kept falling down, the king called Merlin, the magician, to find out why. Merlin determined that there were two dragons fighting in a pool beneath the site. Think it's just an old story? Check out the ruined temple today where it still (sort of) stands on Salisbury plain. It is called Stonehenge....

*wink!*

It's often said that English mapmakers used to write "Here Be Dragons" at the edges of their maps to mark the **ends of the known world.** But experts say that these legendary words didn't exist any more than the dragons did. (They appear on only one map!)

80

# THE HENHAM DRAGON

It was 1668, another quiet day in the British village of Henham, Essex. But not for long. Suddenly, a horrible creature appeared in the sky. It was nine feet long, with oddly small wings. Its eyes were surrounded by feathers. Some villagers only caught a glimpse of it in the distance. Others got a closer look, reporting that they saw the dragon flying directly overhead.

The Henham dragon quickly became a sensation. In 1669, it was described in a booklet called *The Flying Serpent or Strange News Out of Essex*. Seven people, including the local church warden, swore that everything in the pamphlet was true. It wasn't until 1990—nearly 330 years after its appearance—that the Henham dragon was revealed to be an elaborate hoax. William Winstanley, a local Henham man, had built a nine-foot-long wood and canvas dragon model. He and his seven pals wrote up the story and printed the pamphlet. Why? Well, it seems it was 1668, and just another quiet day in the British village of Henham, Essex....

# DRAGONS IN SPACE...

In both Eastern and Western mythology, the dragon is considered to be the enemy of the sun and the moon. **Eclipses**, it was thought, were caused by the dragons trying to eat the celestial bodies.

**Are you a dragon?** You are if you were born in 1988 or 2000. According to the Chinese calendar, these were the two most recent years of the Dragon, which occur every 12 years. Being born in a Dragon year gives you extraordinary abilities, including powerful ambition and the gift of the gab.

You can find a dragon in the sky every night! The constellation Draco is best seen in the Northern Hemisphere in the month of July at around nine o'clock at night.

The word "typhoon" comes from Typhon, the name of a fire-breathing monster in Greek myths. The story goes that Typhon created rivers by gouging out parts of the earth during a battle with Zeus. The word "hurricane" comes from the dragon world too. Huracan is the name of a mythical winged serpent that's native to the Caribbean. No wonder dragons are frequently used as a symbol of the changing seasons.

This picture shows how to find Draco in the night sky—in relation to the Big Dipper.

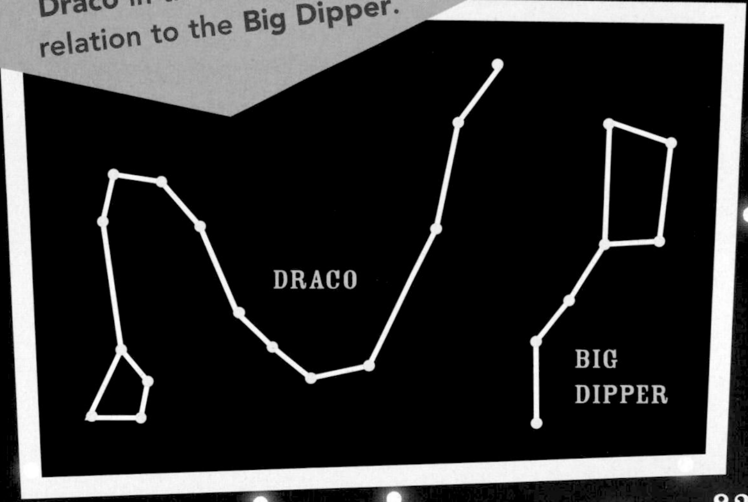

DRACO

BIG DIPPER

# Those Crafty Dragons!

## The Disappearing Dragon

**D**id you ever wonder why almost no one ever sees a dragon—especially since they are so big? The reason is partly dragon magic, and partly clever camouflage. To see how dragons hide in plain sight, try this spellbinding experiment.

### YOU'LL NEED
2 pieces of dark blue or black poster board
**pencil**
**white correction liquid or white poster paint**
**a small paintbrush**
**scissors • masking tape**
**a hand mirror • a friend**

84

1. Using the picture here as a guide, draw a large dragon on one piece of the poster board. Leave enough room below to draw in the "handle" (see step 2).

2. Add a handle to your dragon by drawing a long rectangle, about 20 cm (8 in.) long and 7.5 cm (3 in.) wide, running from the dragon's belly to the bottom of the paper.

20 CM (8 IN.) LONG

3. Using the correction fluid or poster paint, make tiny white dots all over both sheets of board. The dot pattern should be random, but similar on both sheets. Think of lots of tiny dazzling stars against a dark sky. Let dry.

4. Cut out your dragon with its handle. Fly it around the room, making some nice dragony roaring sounds, just for fun.

5. Fasten the sheet of poster board at eye level to the wall with small pieces of masking tape. (Get permission from your parents before you do this—the tape can mark some walls.)

6. Have your friend hold the dragon cut-out very still about 15 cm (6 in.) in front of the dotted sheet.

7. Take about eight steps away from the wall. Keep your back to your friend and hold up the hand mirror. Look into the mirror, adjusting its position until you can see the dotted board. Can you spot the spotted dragon?

8. Switch places so your friend can have a chance to seek the beast too.

**Tip:** The trick is to hold the dragon very, very still. As soon as the dragon moves, its camouflage spell will weaken and you will be able to glimpse it. Now comes the hard part—not letting the dragon see you!

### HOW DOES IT WORK?

The same way that wearing camouflage clothing would help you hide in the jungle. The spotty pattern on the dragon is close enough to the spots on the background to blend together in your eye. Unless you are in very bright light, the dragon's outline disappears against the dark backdrop. Until the dragon moves, it's practically invisible. To human eyes, anyway. Fairy eyes can see dragons no problem.

# Mother Goose GETS DOWN on the FARM

CHICKEN LITTLE'S FARMYARD

PIGGY 1

PIGGY 2

PROPERTY OF LITTLE BOY BLUE

OLD MACDONALD'S FARM

MARY'S OBEDIENCE SCHOOL

## TRAVEL NOTES:

The southern provinces of Happilyeverafter are primarily rural. This bucolic region is made up of pastures, meadows, and working farmland. Principal crops include magically growing **beans** and **pumpkins**. Exceptional sheep, billy goats gruff, dairy cows, and poultry are also raised.

Delightful experiences await the visitor. Enjoy regional specialties such as Little Boy Blue Haystacks, and 101 varieties of **scrambled Humpty Dumpty egg**. The rolling countryside is a treat for the eye. Quaint thatched cottages made of straw and sticks will enchant.

While tales of mice over-running the farms have kept some visitors away in the past, today's traveler can rest assured that humane measures are being taken to keep the **rodent population** under control.

Visitors are asked to be on the lookout for **Little Bo Peep's sheep**. She's lost her flock—again!—and doesn't know where to find them. Report any sightings to the Bureau of Missing Animals.

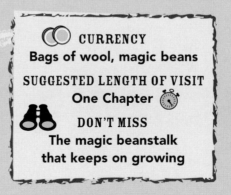

**CURRENCY**
Bags of wool, magic beans

**SUGGESTED LENGTH OF VISIT**
One Chapter

**DON'T MISS**
The magic beanstalk that keeps on growing

IGGY 3

JACK'S BEAN GARDEN

Hello, dahlings

# Nursery Rhymes:

## THE INSIDE STORY

Just who is Mother Goose? Mother Goose stories have been around for a long time—since at least 1650. By 1697, a goose wearing a bonnet was pictured in a French collection of fairy tales. She crossed the English Channel shortly afterwards, and began appearing in puppet shows. By the early 1800s, she was well known to English children as well.

John Newbery's classic book **Mother Goose's Melody: or Sonnets for the Cradle** made Mother Goose an international star. English-speaking kids all over the world became familiar with Mother Goose's characters, including dishes that ran away with spoons, boys who jumped over candlesticks, and contrary young misses named Mary.

Some people think that the words for **Ring-Around-the-Rosie** actually describe the progress of the Black Plague, a deadly disease that swept across Europe during the Middle Ages.

**Jack Be Nimble** may have been trying to see his future. In England, it was seen as good luck if a person could jump over a lit candle without the flame going out.

You know how Baa Baa Black sheep claims to have **three bags of wool**? The division of wool into three bags was due to a tax set on wool in 1275.

Next time there's a full moon, see if you can spot "**Jack and Jill**" carrying a pail of water. A Scandinavian myth says that the dark spots you see are the two children captured by the moon.

**Little Bo-Peep** began her life as the game you know as Peek-a-Boo! In olden days, it was called—you guessed it—Bo-Peep.

While most nursery rhymes known today date from the 1700s, a version of "I'm the king of the castle..." from Ancient Roman times is more than 2,000 years old!

## Dirty Dish Tales

91

# Mother Goose's Duck-tionary

**N**ot every word means the same thing on Mother Goose's farm as you'd expect. This brand gnu guide has all the latest lingo you'll need.

Quack!

**ADDER**—plus-sized serpent

**ALPACA**—what you say before you leave on a trip; for example, "Alpaca sweater, you pack a hat."

**ANTELOPE**—what insects do when they want to marry

**BELIEVER**—a bee leaving the hive, of course

**CARIBOUSTER**—elk cheerleader

**CATAPULT**—feline tossing device; used for "raining cats and dogs"

**COATI**—South American rodent, related to the jacketi and mittensi

**DUCK-TIONARY**—a book covered in feathers that quacks out word definitions

**DINGO**—wild canines; relatives of B-I-N-G-O

**DODO**—two female deer

**DUCT TAPE**—very sticky adhesive; used for repairing quacks

**DUST MITE**—mascot animal of indifferent housekeepers (they just might dust, they just might not...and don't even get them started on vacuuming!)

**GULLIBLE**—believes every word uttered by seagulls

**ELEPHANTASY**—dreaming of pink pachyderms in tutus

**HAREBALL**—rabbit rolling down a hill

**HOARSE**—a colt with a sore throat

**MILKSHAKE**—dancing cow

**MOOVERS AND SHAKERS**—cows that make things happen

**OSTRICH**—a wealthy bird

**PANDEMIC**—worldwide outbreak of excessive cuteness in pandas

**PIGPENMANSHIP**—sloppy handwriting

**ROBIN**—untrustworthy thief of the bird world

**RODENTITION**—buck teeth

**SPIDER**—arachnid secret agent

**WOMBAT**—1: opposite of a chilly bat; 2: Sporting equipment used for playing womball

# Hey Diddle RIDDLES

What did Baa Baa Black Sheep say to Mary's Little Lamb at the field gate?

**After ewe!**

What do you call a rooster that can't find its voice?

**Cock-a-doodle-don't.**

What has 12 legs, three tails, and six eyes but can't see?

**Three blind mice!**

What do cows use to subtract?

**Cow-culators.**

What happened when the clock struck one?

**The rest of the mice got away with minor injuries.**

smack!

eep!

Run away! Run away!

94

Why did the cow cross the road?

**To get to the udder side!**

What would you get if you crossed Bo Peep's littlest sheep with a karate expert?

**Lamb chops.**

What would you get if you crossed the ugly duckling with the cow that jumped over the moon?

**Milk and quackers.**

How did the farmer in the dell fix the hole in his jeans?

**With a cabbage patch!**

What's a pig's favorite ballet?

**Swine Lake.**

Why does a rooster watch TV?

**For hen-tertainment.**

How do you take a pig to hospital?

**By hambulance.**

What did the cow study before its math test?

**Moo-tiplication tables.**

What do you give a sick pig?

**Oinkment.**

What do you get if you cross a chicken with a cement mixer? **A brick-layer!**

95

# Meet

# Little Miss Muffet's Spider

Miss Muffet was surprised when a spider crawled up beside her. Your friends will be too when you make this spooky eight-legged climber.

## YOU'LL NEED

cardboard • pencil • scissors
crayons or markers • 4 black pipe cleaners
tape • 1 drinking straw • ruler
string, 1m (3 ft.) long

1 On the cardboard, draw a large circle (approximately 15 cm/6 in.) joined with a smaller circle on top (see below). This is your spider's head and body.

**2** Cut out the spider. Color one side in a spiderlike way—scary is good!

**3** Turn your spider over so the colored side is face down. Tape the four pipe cleaners horizontally across the spider's body. Bend the top two pipe cleaners to make four legs facing upwards; bend the bottom two pipe cleaners to make four legs facing downwards.

**4** Cut two 2.5 cm (1 in.) long pieces from the straw. Tape them—about 2.5 cm (1 in.) apart—to the abdomen of the spider as shown.

**5** Fold your string in half. Working from the head, slip one end of the string through one of the straws. Slip the other end through the other straw. You should now have a loop of string sticking out above the spider's head, and two long string tails hanging down from its bottom.

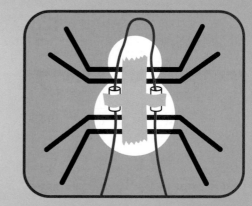

**6** To put your spider into action, hang the loop over a doorknob or a hook conveniently near your "victim." Hold the string ends in each hand; your spider should be down near your hands.

**7** Gently pull the two loose string ends down and away from each other. The spider will magically climb up the strands of its "web!"

# Old Macdonald's Dog

YOU ALL KNOW OUR NEXT PERFORMER, SO GIVE HIM A BIG HAND.

LET'S HEAR IT FOR JOHN JACOB JINGLEHEIMER SCHMIDT!

OLD MACDONALD HAD A FARM, AND BINGO WAS HIS NAME-O....

EXCUSE ME, MR. SCHMIDT, BUT THAT'S NOT RIGHT!

HUH?

THE FARMER'S NAME ISN'T BINGO, SIR. HIS NAME IS FRED. FRED MACDONALD. HIS DOG IS NAMED BINGO.

REALLY? SO SORRY. MY MISTAKE.

AHEM...AND ON THAT FARM HE HAD SOME CHICKS...

ER, EXCUSE ME, BUT THAT'S NOT RIGHT! THE CHICKENS ALL CLEARED OFF MACDONALD'S FARM THE DAY CHICKEN LITTLE DISCOVERED THE SKY WAS FALLING.

REALLY? SO SORRY. MY MISTAKE AGAIN.

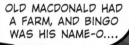

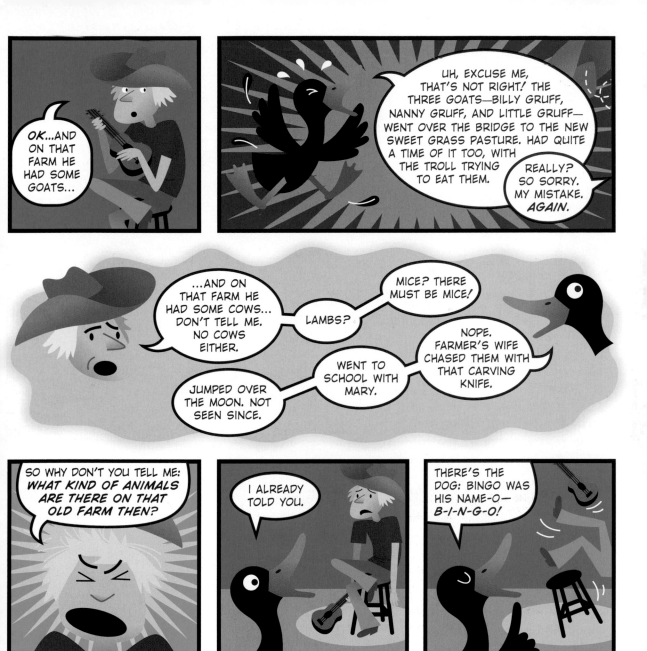

# BUILDING A BETTER
# Mousetrap

## Better Mousetrap #73:

Dog (A) barks loudly to be let out. Startled nearby cat (B) faints, falling onto lever (C), which knocks toy car (D) down the stairs. Toy car bumps into bucket (E) on the stairs, so that it knocks into electrical switch (F), turning on fan (G). A helium balloon (H) buried under the laundry in basket (I) escapes and rises up in the air. String attached to balloon is wrapped around enticing chunk of cheese (J). Fan blows balloon so cheese dangles above mouse-hole (K). Mouse (L), lured out by the aroma, leaps at cheese. With teeth firmly in cheese (which is still fastened to balloon) mouse is blown toward door. Door, meanwhile, has been opened to let out dog with bursting bladder. Mouse's hot air balloon ride carries it far from farm.

The Farmer's Wife is sick and tired of chasing those mice around the house. Besides, she's really not that cruel a gal—even *she* thinks the carving knife is not really necessary. What she'd like best of all is for those mice to leave her humble home. For good.

So Fannie Farmer, being a clever and creative type, has put on her thinking cap to invent a better mousetrap. She has come up with hundreds of wacky inventions (one for each of the pesky mice). Here are two of the best. She hopes these will end her pest problem forever.

## Better Mousetrap #109:

Mouse appears at mousehole (A). Lady (B), seeing mouse, shrieks. Shriek reaches high note, causing glass (C) on table to break. Glass shards land on windowsill (D), where sunlight falls upon them causing reflected light to bounce up at ice cube (E) suspended from ceiling by tongs (F). As ice melts, water droplets fall into funnel (G). Droplets run through funnel into attached hose (H) suspended over pail (I), attached to pulley (J). As pail fills, it pulls down on pulley, causing hook (K) on other side of pulley to release large pot lid (L), which drops onto pile of pots and pans (M) below. Mouse (N), fed up with all the noise, packs bag and leaves for the city.

N — I am *so* out of here!

Eeek!

# Recipes from the

## "Sat Down Beside Her" Spiders

**Miss Muffet wasn't frightened for long. She came back with a net and captured that spider. It was delish! Taste the spider for yourself with this easy recipe.**

### YOU'LL NEED
**large round crackers**
**peanut butter***
**chocolate chips**
**mini-pretzel sticks**

### YOU'LL ALSO NEED
**knife**

1. Spread peanut butter on one cracker.
2. Arrange eight pretzel sticks coming off the cracker but sticking on the peanut butter to make the eight legs of the spider.
3. Place a second cracker on top to make a sandwich.
4. Using two dabs of peanut butter as "glue," stick two chocolate chips on the top—these will be the spider's eyes.

**Yield:** make as many spiders as you have guests

**Prep time:** 10 minutes

***ALTERNATIVE:** If you are allergic to peanuts, substitute marshmallow spread, cream cheese, or jelly for the peanut butter.

# Fairy Tale Farm

## Little Boy Blue Haystacks

**Little Boy Blue fell asleep in his haystack. You can eat yours.**

### YOU'LL NEED

**1 10 oz. package of butterscotch chips**

**125 mL (1/2 cup) peanut butter***

**325 mL (1 1/3 cup) chow mein style noodles**

### YOU'LL ALSO NEED

**pot**
**2 mixing spoons**
**waxed paper**
**cookie sheet**
**teaspoon**
**spatula**

1. Ask a grownup for help with steps 1 to 3. Melt the butterscotch chips (and the marshmallows, if using) in a pot over medium heat on the stove, about 5 minutes.

2. Stir in the peanut butter (or marshmallow spread, if using).

3. Add the chow mein noodles. Stir until they are completely coated. Remove the pot from the heat.

4. Cover the cookie sheet with a sheet of waxed paper. Using a mixing spoon, scoop out about 5 mL (1 teaspoon) of the mixture. Use the other spoon to push the gooey stuff into a little haystack on the waxed paper. Repeat, using up all the mixture.

5. Let cool before eating. An hour in the fridge should do it!

**Yield:** 12 haystacks (depending on how big each one comes out)

**Prep time:** 30 minutes

***ALTERNATIVE:** If you are allergic to peanut butter, substitute 125 mL (1/2 cup) marshmallows or marshmallow "fluff" spread.

103

# Nutty Nursery Rhymes

## Mixed-Up Kid

Peter Piper wore a diaper
Like a bonnet on his head
And where he sat
He wore a hat,
To keep his backside warm, he said

## ...Tumbling After

Dear daffodil
Upon the hill,
Have you seen
Young Jack and Jill?

They can't be far
(They have no car)
Bonk-a-bonk
Well, here they are!

## The Absent-Minded Shepherdess

Little Bo Peep has lost her sheep,
Her sweater and her shoe,
Her backpack, lunch,
and homework notes,
And, yes, her mind (it's true!)

## Mooops!

The cow jumped over the moon
And crashed right into Mars
She shook her head, blinked once
and mooed,
"By Jove! I'm seeing stars!"

SEARCH:
sheep

# for Modern Children

## Mean Queen Cole

Old King Cole was a merry old soul
But the queen was a bit of a pain
So he called for his coach
And he called for his cloak
Never came to his castle again!

## The Fishmonger's Lament

Why, oh why,
Put birds in a pie
When tarts made from fish
Are quite moist and delish?

## A Mouse Tale

Hickory, dickory, dock!
The mouse ran up my sock
On my shin it did chew
Then fell into my shoe
Sniffed my toes and got a rude shock

## Smelly, Smelly Cinderelly

Smelly, smelly Cinderelly
Turned the prince to royal jelly
When he caught a whiff of her
Pungent underarm *odeur*

Gassed by Cindy's potent charms
He swooned into her ample arms
And as the luckless royal fell
He succumbed to her ripe smell

The slipper sealed the prince's fate
When his aromatic date
Stuck her stinky foot in it
And, alas, the slipper fit!

So the prince and Cindy wed
But soon the smell killed
that prince dead
And that's the tale I have to telly
Of smelly, smelly Cinderelly

# PICTURE THESE WORDS

**C**an you solve these tricky picture–word puzzles based on favorite nursery rhymes? You'll need a piece of paper and a pencil. Where there's a picture, write out the name of the object on your own paper (psst—spelling counts!). Add or subtract letters as directed. If you do each step correctly, you will be able to match up the solutions to the following four questions:

**1** Who jumped over a candlestick?

**2** Who scolded the kittens for losing their mittens?

**3** What did the Grand Old Duke of York march up the hill and down again?

**4** What did one little piggy have?

Check your answers on page 159.

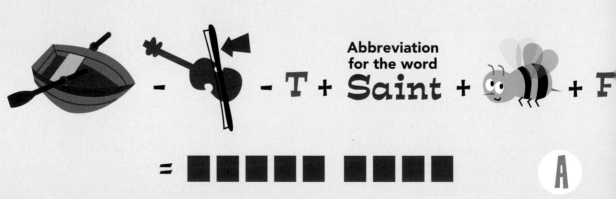

– ![] – T + Abbreviation for the word **Saint** + ![] + F = ▪▪▪▪▪ ▪▪▪▪

**A**

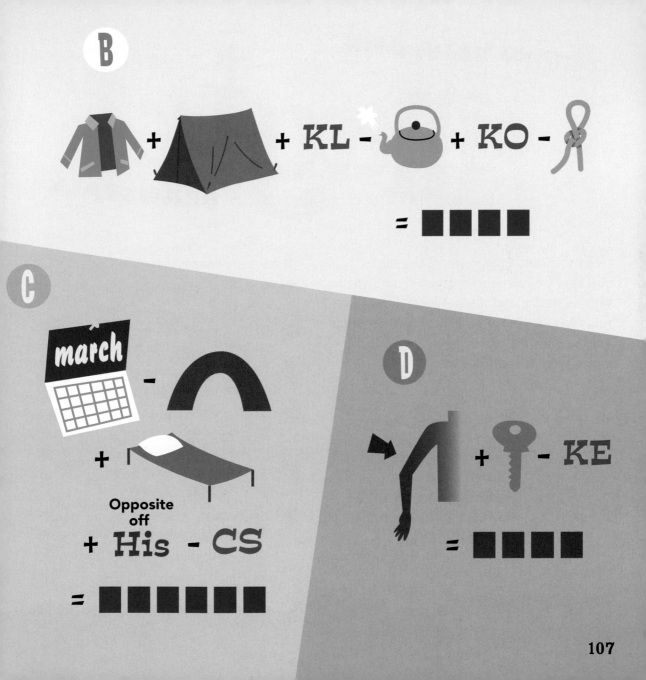

107

# GROW YOUR OWN Magic BEANSTALK

**W**hy should Jack have all the fun? You don't even need a green thumb to grow a beanstalk of your own. It's easy and fun. And just remember that a little magic happens inside plants every time sunshine and water get together (see right).

## YOU'LL NEED
10 cm (4 in.) plastic pot
with drainage holes in the bottom

plastic saucer

potting soil

water

beans (garden varieties from a seed package, not from a food source)

1 Place the saucer under the pot.

2 Fill the pot about halfway up with potting soil.

3 Place six to eight beans in the pot. The beans should not touch each other.

4 Cover the beans with soil. Gently pat down with your finger.

5 Water lightly to dampen the soil. You've watered enough when just a few drips leak out from the bottom of the pot.

6 Check the pot daily. If the soil becomes dry, water again.

7 In a few days, you might see the bean sprouts starting to poke through the soil. Keep the soil moist but not soggy.

8  In a few more days, you may see the first pair of leaves on several of the sprouts. When more pairs of leaves form, thin the seedlings to two or three of the strongest and tallest looking plants. (This means pull out all the others. Gently—so you don't pull out the whole lot by accident.)

9  If the soil outside is completely warm, and there is no danger of frost, you can transplant your seedlings from the pot to the garden. Your seedlings will grow best in a location where there is sun for more than half the day and where the soil does not remain soggy all day long.

HAIR

FEET    CORN    BEANS    TOMATOES

# Green Magic

Inside the leaves of every green plant are tiny chemical factories called *chloroplasts*. They take energy from sunlight and convert it into food in a process called photosynthesis. The word photosynthesis comes from two Greek words that mean "light" (*photo*) and "make" (*synth*). No living thing other than green plants can create its own food. And all other living things depend on the food energy that's created by plants from sunlight. What happens inside those chloroplasts really is magic—it's the magic at the root of life itself!

# Help Humpty!

## YOU'LL NEED
tracing paper

pencil

scissors

cardboard, construction paper, or regular bond paper

**1** Trace all of the egg pieces (below). Cut the shapes out of the tracing paper, then trace all the shapes onto a stronger piece of paper (your cardboard, construction, or regular bond paper). Cut them out.

**2** Scramble up the pieces. Then reassemble them into an egg. Humpty thanks you.

If you're stumped, check page 159 to see Humpty put back together again.

**P**oor Humpty. Those king's men try and try to put Humpty back together, but with no luck. You, however, have what it takes to save the day. Don't you?

# Even More Fun with Humpty

The cool thing about an egg is that when it cracks open, a baby bird usually hatches. So once you have finished putting Humpty Dumpty together, you can reuse the pieces of his egg to make lots of different birdies from famous nursery rhymes.

**Check out the pictures below of some of your favorite feathered fairy tale friends. Can you put them together? Solutions on page 159.**

Goosey Goosey Gander

Blackbird (from the pie)

Cock Robin

Cock-a-Doodle-Doo

Poll Parrot

Swan

Crow

# CAPTAIN SCIENCE meets Humpty Dumpty

The entire tragedy could have been avoided if...sigh...if only Humpty Dumpty had been able to bounce. You, oh Great Magician, can make it so. All you need is the miracle of science. Luckily, we happen to have it right here in this egg-ceptional eggs-periment.

## YOU'LL NEED

1 egg

crayon

500 mL (2 cups) vinegar

glass jar with lid, large enough to hold the egg and vinegar

1 With the crayon, carefully draw a face on the outside of your egg. You now have turned the egg into Humpty Dumpty. Talk to him, and wish him luck. You are about to drown him in vinegar.

2 Place the egg gently into the jar. Wave bye-bye.

3 Pour the vinegar over the egg. The egg has to be completely covered or this eggs-periment won't work. Cover with the lid.

4 In just a few minutes, you might see tiny bubbles start to form around Humpty. This is a good sign. You may also see his carefully drawn face melt away (on the other hand, it might sit tight—depends on your crayon). Oh, well, becoming break-proof has its price.

Wheeee!

Look at me! I'm invincible!

## What's going on?

Eggshells contain a chemical called calcium carbonate. The vinegar reacts with the calcium carbonate, dissolving the shell. (The gas bubbles you saw were carbon dioxide—a sign of the chemical reaction happening right before your eyes.)

Once the shell is gone, the vinegar can pass into the egg. Another chemical reaction takes place, this time between the vinegar and the proteins of the egg white. The vinegar, in effect, "cooks" the egg white. It becomes bouncy—more like a cooked egg than a raw one.

5 Leave Humpty to soak in the vinegar for three whole days.

6 Check on the egg. Does the shell feel soft? If so, gently remove your pal from the vinegar bath.

7 Give him a low bounce on your work surface. Try to bounce the egg from about 7.5 cm (3 in.). How high can you make Humpty hurdle? Boing! Boing! Hooray for Humpty! Hooray for the magic of science!

My sister
(*sniff*) told me
I was (*sniff*)...
UGLY!

# Ugly Duckling Origami

Fold your own ugly duckling,
then transform it into a gorgeous swan!

## YOU'LL NEED

**large square of origami paper***

*Origami begins with a perfectly square piece of paper. Origami paper works best, and can be found at an art supply, craft, or toy store. Regular bond paper will work too, but must be made into a perfect square.

Fold as follows to make your duckling—and then transform it into a swan.

**1** Fold the paper on a diagonal, then unfold to make a crease.

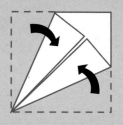

**2** Fold both sides in to the fold. Your shape will resemble a kite.

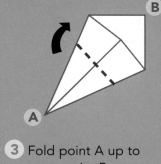

**3** Fold point A up to meet point B.

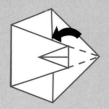

**4** Fold the tip of the paper down to make the duckling's beak.

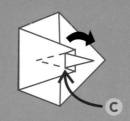

**5** Bend the folded tip backwards from the imaginary line C.

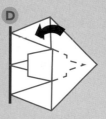

**6** Fold bent tip to meet the edge at line D.

**7** Fold paper in half.

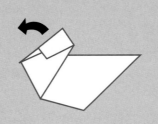

**8** Pull the head and neck gently away from the body. Flatten.

**9** Fold the top layer up to make wings. Repeat on the back side.

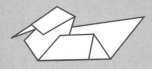

**10** You have finished your ugly duckling! Now turn into a swan.

**11** Hold the body; unfold the head and neck upwards. Flatten.

**12** Create the swan's head by folding the tip down. Flatten.

# Loosey Goosey's Hinky Pinkys

Loosey Goosey, one of Chicken Little's pals, loves a type of rhyming puzzle called Hinky Pinkys. In these puzzles, the answer is always two rhyming words. For example:

**A nickname for a fairy who needs a bath:**
Stinky Tinky

Unfortunately, Loosey Goosey isn't very good at solving puzzles. Can you solve these Hinky Pinkys for Loosey Goosey? (Answers on page 159.)

the mess in the chicken pen

security for the barn

dog's bark

magical being who milks cows

portly puss-in-boots

hag who's a tattle tale

fire-breathing lizard's cart

ailing fowl

nearby lollipop

goofy goat

married rodent

clever song

seat for a bunny

hairpiece for porky

eager royal

swamp of spaniels

plump primate

ill-behaved boy

**TURKEY LURKEY'S
BIG BUCK-BUCK-BUCKS CHALLENGE:**

Can you come up with your own Hinky Pinkys?

117

# Baa Baa Brain Teasers

## THE MAGIC CARPET CHALLENGE

The queen has a magic carpet that can grant your every wish. Before it will do so, however, it must be cut into 11 pieces. The trick is you may use only four cuts, and all of them have to be straight lines. The pieces can be any shape or size.

Are you brave enough to take the queen up on her challenge? If you fail, you will be sent to the dungeons forever. Beat the odds by testing your skill first, before you try it out on the real carpet.

On a piece of paper, draw a rectangle to represent the carpet. Can you divide the carpet into the 11 needed pieces by drawing only four lines to get your every wish granted? Be careful—the dungeon is a cold, drafty place!

**HINT:** Look carefully and you will see a faint fold line on the carpet. This might be a clue to where to place your first line!

## TWINKLE, TWINKLE LITTLE STAR CHALLENGE

```
*   *   *   *   *

*   *   *   *   *

*   *   *   *   *

*   *   *   *   *

*   *   *   *   *
```

Copy this star pattern onto a piece of paper. What is the largest number of squares you can draw in which:

the center star falls inside the boundaries of the square
**AND**
all four corners of the square fall on a star?

118

The great scholars of the Fairy Tale farms—Chicken Little and Co.—have been stumped by these brainteasers posed by the Evil Queen. Can you figure out the solutions and save the day? Check your answers on page 159.

# GRANDMA'S HOUSE PUZZLER

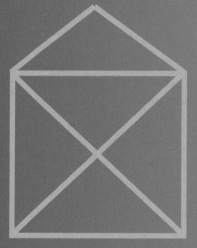

Study the picture of Grandma's house at right. On a separate piece of paper, can you draw the house without:

lifting your pencil from the paper
**AND**
letting any lines cross one another?

# SEVEN DWARVES CHALLENGE

The queen assigned each dwarf a secret number from 0-6. From the following equations, can you figure out which dwarf was assigned which number? Hint to get you started: Dopey is 0 and Happy is 4.

**Dopey + Bashful + Doc = Happy**

**Dopey + Doc + Happy = Sleepy**

**Dopey+ Sneezy + Happy = Grumpy**

119

Play this cooperative game with one, two, or three pals for fun on the run.

## YOU'LL NEED

**1 marker per player (for example, different colored buttons, or game pieces from another game)**

**10 dimes**

**pencap**

**1 die**

**1** Place the pen cap on the central circle, pointing directly at one row of squares—it's the Farmer's Wife's carving knife.

**2** The markers are mice. Put your marker on one of the four mouseholes.

**3** The dimes are wedges of cheese. Scatter the dimes, one per box, anywhere on the game board.

**4** The mice work together to get all the cheese back to the mouseholes without being captured.

**5** To play, mice roll the die to move in a clockwise direction along the path of the spiral towards the center.

**6** If a mouse lands on a space with a cheese wedge, the mouse turns around. On his next turn, he begins heading back to his hole, taking the cheese with him, and leaving it at his hole. Mice can carry only one piece of cheese at any time.

**7** If a mouse makes it to the Farmer's Wife, he gets a free roll. He turns around to head back to his hole, now moving counter-clockwise.

**8** Mice who arrive back at their hole with a cheese get a free roll, starting back again in a clockwise direction to get more cheese.

**9** If a mouse lands in the row that the knife is pointing to, he is removed from play and put in the central circle with the Farmer's Wife.

**10** A mouse can be rescued by another mouse that reaches the Farmer's Wife safely. The rescued mouse can roll out his next turn and begin to head back to his hole.

**11** If a mouse lands on an arrow, beware! The Farmer's Wife is on the move! Rotate the knife in the arrow direction by one row. Any mice in that row go to the Farmer's Wife!

# Run, and Run, and Run!

## TRAVEL NOTES:

No visit to Happilyeverafter would be complete without a visit to Ye Olde Towne. The historic city center retains most of its original architecture. **Cobbled streets** and narrow half-timbered buildings charmingly recall "once upon a time."

Stroll down fabled Drury Lane, where you may meet the Muffin Man and have the chance to savor **baked goods** from the world-renowned Pieman Shoppe. Ye Olde Hat Shoppe (operated by Puss-in-Boots) is always worth a look as well.

The world famous **Farmer's Market**, open Tuesdays and Thursdays, features produce from all corners of Happilyeverafter. Don't miss the pumpkins from Peter's Pumpkin Patch.

A **walking tour** will take you past London Bridge (currently under restoration) and some of the famous homes of Happilyeverafter. Of note are Jack's house and "The Shoe," inhabited by the Old Woman and her numerous offspring. Young ones will enjoy the **crazy twisted rooms**, sloping floors, and sliding stairs of the famous Crooked House.

**CURRENCY**
**Pounds and Pence**

**SUGGESTED LENGTH OF VISIT**
**One Chapter**

**DON'T MISS**
**The Olde Towne Games**

# Goofy Goose TONGUE TWISTERS

If you enjoy tongue twisters, you'll be right at home in Happilyeverafter. Why, Mother Goose has been getting giggles since once upon a time with her perfectly peculiar verses.

Test your talent on these oldies but goodies. Get out a timer and challenge your friends to see who can say each rhyme:

- the fastest
- with the fewest mistakes
- with the funniest mistakes

Swan swam over the sea,
Swim, swan, swim!
Swan swam back again
Well swum, swan!

I need not your needles, they're needless to me;
For kneading of noodles, 'twere needless, you see;
But did my neat knickers but need to be kneed,
I then should have need of your needles indeed.

Peter Piper picked a peck of pickled peppers.
A peck of pickled peppers, Peter Piper picked.
If Peter Piper picked a peck of pickled peppers,
Where's the peck of pickled peppers Peter Piper picked?

Robert Rowley rolled a round roll round.
A round roll Robert Rowley rolled round;
Where rolled the round roll Robert Rowley rolled round?

Betty Botter had some butter,
"But," she said, "this butter's bitter.
If I bake this bitter butter,
it would make my batter bitter.
But a bit of better butter—
that would make my batter better."

So she bought a bit of butter,
better than her bitter butter,
and she baked it in her batter,
and the batter was not bitter.
So 'twas better Betty Botter
bought a bit of better butter.

When a twister a-twisting will twist him a twist,
For the twisting of his twist, he three twines doth intwist;
But if one of the twines of the twist do untwist,
The twine that untwisteth untwisteth the twist.
Untwirling the twine that untwisteth between,
He twirls, with his twister, the two in a twine;
Then twice having twisted the twines of the twine,
He twitcheth the twice he had twined in twain.
The twain that in twining before in the twine,
As twines were intwisted he now doth untwine;
Twist the twain inter-twisting a twine more between,
He, twirling his twister, makes a twist of the twine.

## STORY STARTERS

Ready to make up your own Goofy Goose tongue twisters? Try using some of these story starters to get you going.

Silly Sally swiftly shooed seven silly sheep

She sifted thistles through her thistle-sifter

Give me the gift of a grip top sock: a drip-drape, ship-shape, tip-top sock

A Tudor who tooted a flute tried to tutor two tooters to toot

Mr. See owned a saw and Mr. Soar owned a seesaw

Once upon a barren moor, there dwelt a bear, also a boar

Selfish shellfish

125

# The CASE of the CROOKED MAN

Have you heard about the crooked man who walked a crooked mile, had a crooked cat, and lived in a crooked house by a crooked stile? He was recently arrested, for being a crook! But it was all a misunderstanding. The man wasn't crooked at all. It was only an optical illusion.

**To see for yourself how your brain can be fooled, check out the evidence over the next few pages.**

**EXHIBIT A:** Are the red lines straight or crooked? Use a ruler to check for yourself!

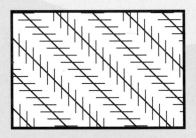

**EXHIBIT B:** Are the long lines crooked, or parallel? Are the short lines all the same length? Get out your trusty ruler, as appearances can be deceiving.

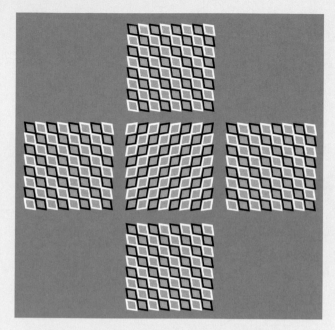

EXHIBIT C: Are the five "blocks" all the same size and shape? What shape are they?

EXHIBIT E: Are the red lines curved or straight?

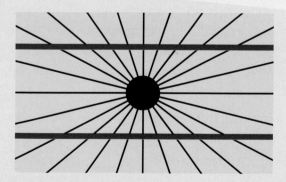

EXHIBIT D: Are the purple lines bowed or parallel?

**EXHIBIT F:** What can you discover about the straight lines that make up the outlines of the letters shown here?

# What's Going On Here?

**OPTICAL ILLUSIONS** happen when your brain receives conflicting information about something you see.

We all rely on basic assumptions to understand the world around us. For example, we learn in infancy that objects that are farther away appear smaller than objects that are close by.

We also know that two parallel lines (like railroad tracks) will look like they get closer and closer together the farther away they are.

Certain images, like the ones on these pages, mess around with those basic assumptions.

128

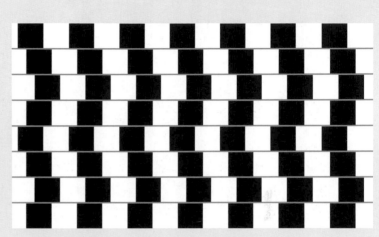

**EXHIBIT G:** Are all the black squares the same size and shape? Are the lines straight or curved?

**EXHIBIT H:** Are the horizontal lines parallel or crooked?

Let's look back at Exhibit D, for example. It's called a Hering Illusion, named after the psychologist who discovered something fishy about lines back in 1861. The lines in Exhibit D are pointing to the central dot. This tells your brain that the dot is far away, like railroad tracks converging in the distance. But it isn't really, is it?

**YOUR BRAIN KNOWS THERE'S A PROBLEM**, but can't quite figure out what it is. In order to make "sense" of the image, your brain mentally bends the purple lines. The image now "works"—even though it's false!

Scientists love optical illusions because they reveal secrets about how our brains work. We just like them because they are fun.

# Mother Goose

## TRIVIA QUIZ

How well do you know your nursery rhymes? Are you a wise old owl when it comes to these childhood favorites, or have you spent too much time at the fair? Check your answers on page 160.

**1** **Who had 27 wigs?**

**a)** Tillie Tiggs

**b)** Gregory Griggs

**c)** Petticoat Pig

**d)** Dapper Don

**2** **Who is the black sheep's second bag of wool for?**

**a)** Mister Woolly

**b)** my dame

**c)** the little boy

**d)** Mother Hubbard

**3** **Where did Bobby Shaftoe go?**

**a)** to market, to market

**b)** to jail

**c)** to sea

**d)** to Londontown

**4** **How many men did the Grand Old Duke of York have?**

**a)** one thousand

**b)** five thousand

**c)** ten thousand

**d)** six hundred

**5** **Who said the following: "Oh what a good boy am I"?**

**a)** Tommy Tucker

**b)** Little Jack Horner

**c)** Georgie Porgie

**d)** Simple Simon

**6** **What did they use to fix Jack's crown?**

**a)** glue

**b)** gold leaf

**c)** vinegar and brown paper

**d)** willow twigs

130

**7** Why were Tweedle-dum and Tweedle-dee arguing?

a) Tweedle-dee ate the last piece of pie.

b) Tweedle-dee spoiled a rattle.

c) Tweedle-dee pushed Tweedle-dum.

d) Tweedle-dum cheated at a game.

**8** Which grew in Mary, Mary Quite Contrary's garden?

a) violets and roses

b) silver bells and cockle shells

c) blue fairies, blue fairies

d) yesses and nos

**9** Where was the Queen when the four-and-twenty blackbirds flew out of the pie?

a) the counting house

b) in the parlor, eating bread and honey

c) hanging up the clothes

d) singing in the throneroom

**10** What did Tom, Tom the Piper's Son steal?

a) a pig

b) a flute

c) a bun

d) a golden goose

# HOW DID YOU DO?

**1-2 CORRECT:**
*Oh Dear, What Can the Matter Be?*
Come home from the fair, and brush up on your Mother Goose!

**3-4 CORRECT:**
*Ten O'Clock Scholar.*
Not bad for a kid who can't get to school much before noon!

**5-6 CORRECT:**
*Mary's Little Lamb.*
Going to school sure has paid off for you! Well done!

**7-10 CORRECT:**
*Wise Old Owl.*
You're the smartest little birdie in the forest!

131

**Y**ou've heard about how Jack jumped over the candlestick. But do you know why Jack jumped over the candlestick? Because he was playing a game. A really good game. You can play too. Best of all, you can play on your own!

## YOU'LL NEED

**14 coins or markers**

**1** Place a coin on each numbered circle at left. But leave space 5 open (no coin).

**2** Move a coin by jumping over another coin to an empty space. You can only jump in a straight line, and you can only jump a coin that is in the next spot—a spot connected to the jumper by a line. Your first jump, therefore, must be from #12 or #14 into spot #5.

**3** Take away the jumped-over coin.

**4** Keep jumping and taking away coins until you can't move anymore—i.e., there aren't any coins next to each other.

**5** The object of the game is to leave the fewest coins possible on the board.

*Check your score below:*

**5 or more coins left:** try again!

**4 coins:** getting there!

**3 coins:** pretty nimble…

**2 coins:** jumps like a jack rabbit!

**1 coin:** Jumping Jack Flash—you did it!

**1 coin in spot #5:** Jack the Giant Killer!

# This Is the **HOUSE** that **JACK** Built...

...and it's a doozy. You see, Jack is great at jumping over candlesticks, but he's a lousy builder. He made a lot of mistakes when he built his dream house.

Can you find all the mistakes Jack made?
You'll find the answers on page 160.

135

INTERVIEW WITH
the Old Woman Who Lives in a Shoe

OUR SPECIAL GUEST TODAY IS THE AUTHOR OF *SAVING YOUR SOLE: A GUIDE TO LIVING SIMPLY*. PLEASE WELCOME THE OLD WOMAN WHO LIVES IN A SHOE!

Hi, folks!

SO, TELL ME, MS., ER...

THE NAME'S LACEY. LACEY BOOTBOTTOM.

WHY A SHOE, MS. B? COULDN'T YOU FIND A MORE CONVENTIONAL HOME FOR YOUR FAMILY?

WELL, RENT IS AWFUL, DEAR. THE OLD SHOE HOUSE WAS GOING CHEAP.

I SEE. SO HOW DID YOU GET THE SHOE READY FOR YOUR FAMILY?

IT'S A LONG STORY....

TIMES WERE ROUGH. MY SON MARTEN—HE'S A DOCTOR NOW—CAME ACROSS THE SHOE HOUSE ONE DAY WHEN WE WERE JUST ABOUT ON OUR LAST LEGS.

IT WAS DOWN AT THE HEEL BUT I GOT MY *16* ELDEST TO DRAG THE SHOE BY THE LACES TO A PRETTY SPOT NEAR THE RIVER HIGHHEELY.

136

# MIXED-UP FAIRY TALE STORY

You and your pal can be the ones to complete this magical—but incomplete—fairy tale! On a separate piece of paper, write the numbers 1 to 24 down the left side of the page. Next, ask your friend to supply the key words and record them on your paper. Then read out the fairy story at right, filling in the words that your friend supplied that correspond to the brackets.

**YOU'LL NEED**
**a friend**
**paper**
**pencil**

*Write down the key words your friend supplies according to this list:*

**1.** name

**2.** thing

**3.** object

**4.** expression of dismay (eg., "Oh, no!" or "How can that be?")

**5.** adjective (a word that describes something, eg., purple, soft, tired)

**6.** body part

**7.** adjective

**8.** adjective

**9.** animal

**10.** body part

**11.** a greeting (eg., "Hi there!" or "How do you do?")

**12.** animal

**13.** something a criminal might say

**14.** verb (an action word), in the past tense

**15.** another body part

**16.** verb, in the past tense

**17.** another verb in the past tense

**18.** adjective

**19.** something that happens (eg., the flowers grow, my teeth fall out, the dog barks)

**20.** a famous person

**21.** silly object

**22.** verb, in the past tense

**23.** verb, in the past tense

**24.** adjective

138

nce upon a time the Royal Princess <1> was sitting in the palace garden near the royal <2>. She was playing with her royal <3> when she dropped it into the <2>.

"<4>," she said. "I love playing with my <3> in the garden."

Suddenly she heard a <5> sound. Bubbles began to well up from the <2>. A <6> appeared out of the <2>. It belonged to a <7>, <8> <9>! The <9> was wearing a crown on its <10>.

"<11>!" said the <9>. "Did you lose your <3>?"

<1> screamed like a <12> and said, "<13>!"

The <9> <14> and said, "If you want your <3> back, you will have to kiss me on the <15>." The princess <16> and <17>.

That night, <1> said, "You are the most <18> creature I have ever seen. I will kiss you on the <15> when <19>."

The <9> said, "The sooner the better. Not only will you get your <3> back, but I will turn into <20> and make you my wife."

So the princess kissed the <9>. Poof! He turned into a <21>.

"You lied!" cried <1>.

"Not entirely," said the <9>. "You are now my wife. And we will live happily ever after."

At which the princess took the <3>, which had appeared, <22> the <9> over the head with it and <23> away.

And the moral of the story is: Don't believe everything you hear from a <24> <9>.

The End.

# Wee Willie Winkie
# MAP QUEST

Every night, Wee Willie Winkie runs through the town, making sure all the good little boys and girls are in bed. If he comes to a house where a child is up past his or her proper bedtime, he jots down the initial of their first name on his parchment notepad.

One night, when Willie Winkie got back to his own home, he noticed that the initials he had jotted down spelled out some very good advice! To see the advice for yourself, follow the directions below to travel in Willie's footsteps. Write down the letters he collects along the way in your own notepad. Answer on page 160.

1 Go east on Rumpelstiltksin Rd.

2 Turn north on Picklejar Ave.

3 Go west on Avenue B.

4 Head north on Humpty Dumpty Drive.

5 Go east on Pickpocket Alley.

6 Take West Street to Rob Row.

7 Head north on Rapunzel Rd.

8 Travel east on the Garter Beltway.

9 Turn south on A Road and travel around the Ring-Around-a-Rosie in a counter-clockwise direction to No Way.

10 Take the Pie Way to Rat Road.

11 Follow the bend then go south at Gateway Rd.

12 Turn into Old Shorts Rd.

13 Go Northwest on Main Boulevard.

14 Turn West onto South Street.

15 Go south on Fairy Ave.

16 Head west on Oranges & Lemons St.

17 Turn south on Picklejar Avenue.

18 Head east on The Cabbage Row then turn south down Top Hat Road.

19 Go west on Rumpelstiltskin Rd., and back to Wee Willie Winkie's Home.

140

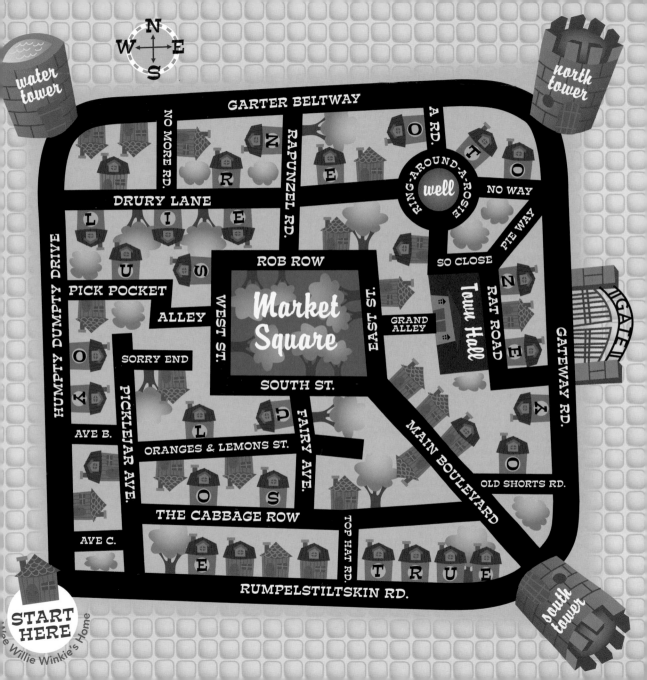

# Recipes from ye

## Humpty Dumpty Scrambled Eggs

### YOU'LL NEED
**4 eggs**
**pinch of salt**
**5 mL (1 teaspoon) butter or margarine**

### YOU'LL ALSO NEED
**mixing bowl**
**fork or small whisk**
**frying pan**
**spatula**

1. Crack the eggs into the mixing bowl. Add a pinch of salt.
2. Use the fork or small whisk to mix the eggs thoroughly.
3. Put the butter or margarine in the frying pan. Have a grown-up help you with this step. Melt the butter in the pan on medium high heat.
4. When the butter is sizzling, carefully pour the eggs into the pan. Let them set slightly, then stir up with the whisk or fork (if your pan is non-stick, use a rubber or silicon spatula that will not scratch the pan).
5. When eggs are mostly set, scrape from the pan onto your plate or bowl. Eat at once!

**Serves:** 2 • **Prep time:** 10 minutes

142

## Pease Porridge Hot
### (a.k.a Split Pea Soup)

### YOU'LL NEED
**500 mL (2 cups) dried split green peas**
**625 mL (2 1/2 cups) water**
**salt and pepper (to taste)**
**croutons (optional)**
**parmesan cheese (optional)**

### YOU'LL ALSO NEED
**measuring cup**
**mixing spoon**
**pot with lid**

**1** Place the water and split peas in the pot. Cover and cook for about an hour on medium-low heat, stirring occasionally to keep peas from sticking to the bottom of the pot. Ask a grown-up for help with the stove and be sure to monitor the soup while the element is on.

**2** When the peas are completely mushy, add salt and pepper to taste.

**3** Serve topped with croutons and a sprinkling of grated parmesan cheese, if desired.

**Serves:** 4 • **Prep time:** just over an hour

# Ye Olde Towne

## Homes for Sale

We're on the level when we say this home is simply one of a kind! Eight crooked rooms include all appliances. Ideal for the handy home repairer. No crooked offers accepted.

Cozy in-town pied-a-terre. Completely cat-proofed.

On the Historic Register! Former home of Peter, Peter Pumpkin Eater's wife! Won't last past Frost.

**OUT-OF-TOWN PROPERTIES:**

Estate Sale! Sweet little cottage set in wooded glen. All modern conveniences, including a super-sized oven.

Family compound near Wolfville features three principal dwellings built from all natural local materials— one in tasteful red brick, one in eco-friendly straw bales, and one in quaint log/sticks. A great getaway retreat for the whole clan!

## Help Wanted

**Domestic Worker.** For small family of mother, and two daughters. Need able-bodied gal to sweep the floors, sew the clothes, serve the food, make the beds, and wash dishes until the wee hours of the morning. Must maintain pleasant attitude in spite of lady of the manor's unrelentingly high standards, daughters' "aristo" manners. Great career opportunity—previous jobholder now living in palace with prince! Call STEPMOTHER 555-SHOE.

**Domestic Worker.** For hanging up clothes in king's garden. Must not be afraid of blackbirds, especially ones that are irritable from having been baked into pies. Pays sixpence a day. Call QUEEN at 555-NOSE.

**Musician.** Must be able to play singing harp. Inquire with Giant.

**Rat Catcher.** Immediate: City overrun! Farmer's Wife preferred but will accept pipers, Puss-in-Boots. Contact Mayor of Hamelin, 1-800-HELP.

## Lost and Found

**Reward offered:** For girl whose foot will fit into glass slipper. Please send foot size, 8 x 10 glossy photo, to Castle.

**Fee** (fi fo fum) **offered:** For finder of Golden Goose. Last

seen in possession of a boy on a beanstalk, and if I find him I'm gonna grind his bones to make my bread!

**Found:** One Black Sheep. Answers to Baa Baa. Call Little Boy Who Lives Down the Lane.

**Lost:** Three pairs mittens. Kittens desperate to retrieve them before mother finds out. Cat's Cradle Lane, Old Towne.

**Found:** One Plum. In Christmas Pudding. Contact Jack Horner, Corner.

145

# The Three Wise Men of Gotham

They may be wise (that is, if going to sea in a bowl is considered wise…) but, alas, no one can understand them! Can you decipher what common words of wisdom these clever fellows are trying to share with the citizens of Olde Towne? Answers on page 160.

An excess of culinary experts impairs the quality of a thin boiled derivative of meat.

A chronic disposition to inquiry deprived the domestic feline of its vitality.

It is not advantageous to place the sum total of your barnyard collections into the same wicker receptacle.

There's no value to be derived from demanding attention by loud screeches over fallen white liquid obtained from the lactic glands of a female bovine.

Three wise men of Gotham    Went to sea in a bowl    And i

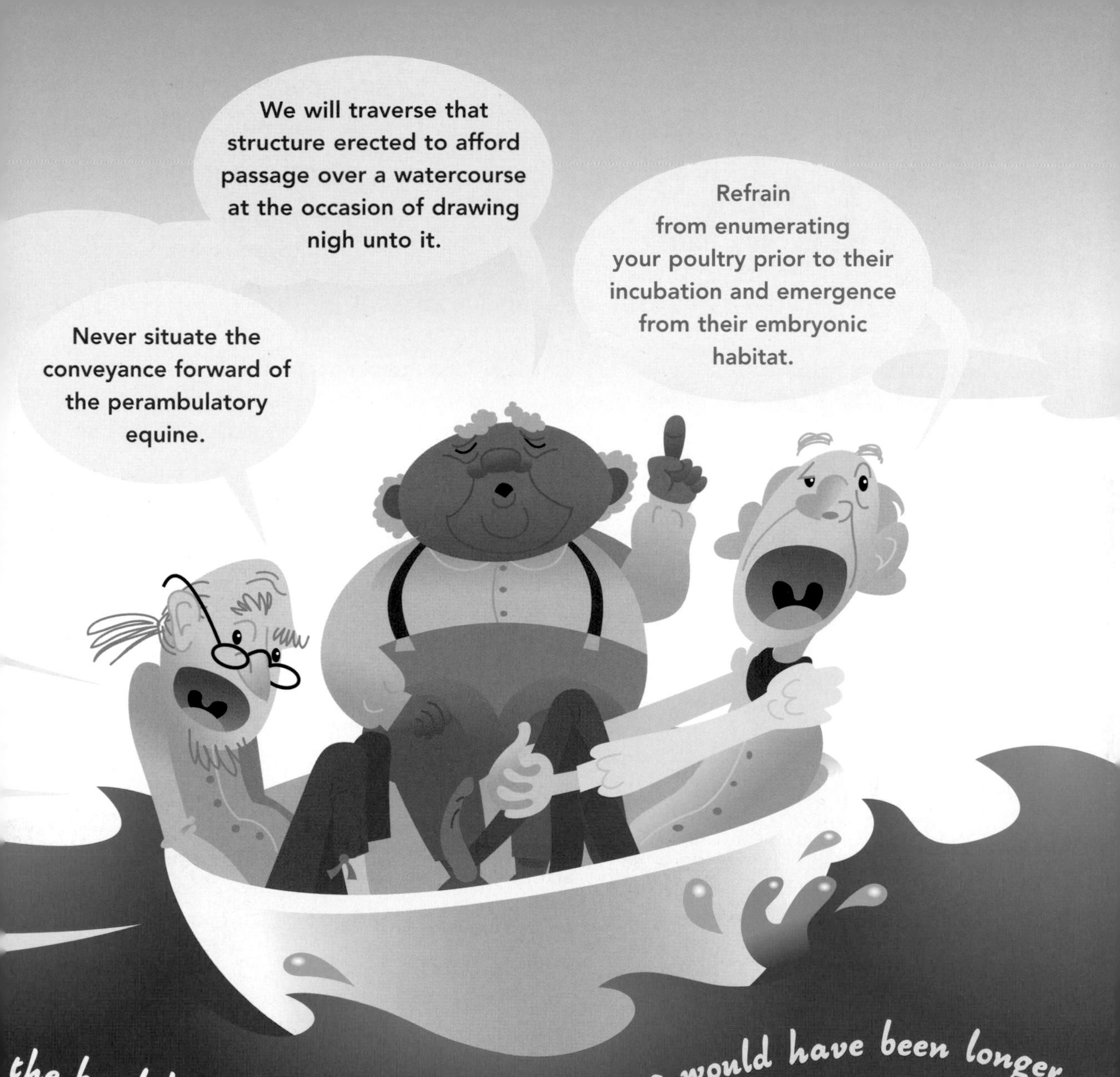


the bowl had been stronger My song would have been longer.

# Olde Towne Games

When they aren't busy jumping over candlesticks or running through the town, fairy tale kids like to play some of these classic outdoor games. Try them out yourself!

## Hit the Pence

**YOU'LL NEED**
**any type of ball (any size)**
**2 or more players**
**a penny**

1. Place the penny on a smooth, hard surface. Have each player stand about 1 m (3 feet) away from the penny, facing each other.

2. The first player bounces the ball so that it (a) hits the penny and (b) bounces up to the other player, who should catch it on the single bounce, if they can. Whoever hits the penny on a single bounce "wins."

3. When **both** players "win," each player takes a large step backwards, then tries again to hit the penny on a bounce to another player. This makes the game harder so you can keep on playing and having fun!

4. For more challenge and excitement, keep score, giving yourselves points for each time you hit the penny, and taking away points for each time you fail to catch the ball on one bounce. The first player to 15 is the winner.

# Castle-Spider Soccer

**soccer ball**
**6–12 players**

1 Choose a flat grassy area free of obstacles for the playing field. Arrange two goals, one at each end of the playing area (about half the length, or less, of a regular soccer field).

2 Divide the players into two teams. Now get all the players down on the ground in spider position, with both feet and both hands on the ground, bottoms facing the ground and tummies facing the sky, so they can move like spiders.

3 The game is otherwise played like ordinary soccer. Players may only use their feet to kick the ball. The first team to score five goals wins.

# Castle Wall Handball

**a tennis ball**
**2 players**
**an outdoor wall**

1 Decide your "court's" boundaries. The first player "serves" the ball by bouncing it once on the ground, then smacking it with his or her palm against the wall.

2 The second player lets the ball bounce once, then smacks it against the wall.

3 Play continues until one player misses the ball or the ball goes out of bounds. Players score points when their opponents miss. The first player to 15 wins.

# Peter, Peter, Pumpkin-Eater vs. the Good Fairy

**P**eter wants the best pumpkin in the pumpkin patch to make a house for his wife. The Good Fairy wants it, however, to make a magic coach for Cinderella. Battle it out to see who gets to grab the really good gourd!

*Three of a Kind*

*Four of a Kind*

*Four in a Row*
(e.g., 1,2,3,4 or 2,3,4,5 or 3,4,5,6)

*Full House*
(2 of one kind, 3 of another, e.g., 2 ones and 3 fours)

150

## YOU'LL NEED

**8 markers**
**(buttons or games pieces)**
**5 dice**
**2 players**

1. Place a marker on each of the pumpkins below.

2. The player with the most buttons on his or her clothing goes first.

3. The object of the game is to collect the most markers. To do so, roll all five dice. Decide which "pumpkin" you want, for example, "Three of a Kind."

4. Say you rolled 2 fours, a two, a three, and a six. Set the 2 fours aside, and re-roll the other three dice to try to wind up with Three of a Kind on your second roll.

5. Still no luck with fours? Roll any or all of the dice one more time (you get three rolls in total per turn).

6. If at any time during your turn you roll one of the combinations that is listed on a pumpkin (it doesn't have to be the one you were angling for), you may take the counter from that pumpkin. You can collect only one counter per turn.

7. Now the second player goes. They will get three tries to roll any combination shown on a pumpkin *for which there is still a counter available.*

8. Continue, alternating turns, until all the counters have been removed from the pumpkin patch.

9. The player with the most markers wins.

*3 Twos*

*3 Threes*

*3 Fives*

*3 Sixes*

151

# What's Your Fairy Tale

If you lived in Happilyeverafter, which famous character would you be? To take this personality test, you'll need a pencil and paper for your answers. Since we all have various personality traits and moods, you may get a different answer on another day. Put your results together to see what fairy tale character combo is you!

**1 When you see mice, you prefer to:**

a) chase them with a carving knife
b) ask them to help you make a dress
c) offer to sell them some cheese

If you chose a), go to question 4. If you chose b), go to question 3. If you chose c), go to question 2.

**2 Do you prefer:**

a) doing something creative
b) cooking
c) working with animals

If you chose a), go to question 8. If you chose b), go to question 6. If you chose c), go to question 10.

**3 Where would you rather live:**

a) in the city, where there is excitement
b) in the forest, where it is peaceful and quiet
c) in a palace, where there is every luxury

If you chose a), go to question 9. If you chose b), go to question 12. If you chose c), go to question 5.

**4 Your favorite food is:**

a) vegetables and fruits
b) meat
c) sweets

If you chose a), go to question 13. If you chose b), go to question 11. If you chose c), go to question 7.

**5 Which appeals to you more:**

a) a fluffy feather bed
b) a gorgeous outfit
c) a magic wand

If you chose a), go to question 18. If you chose b), go to question 14. If you chose c), go to question 21.

**6 Which would you rather eat right now:**

a) a plum
b) a snack
c) sweets

152

# Personality?

If you chose a), you are **Jack Horner**. If you chose b), go to question 22. If you chose c), go to question 7.

## 7 Which is your favorite game:

**a)** tic tac toe
**b)** crazy eights
**c)** tag

If you chose a), go to question 13. If you chose b), you are are the **Queen of Hearts**. If you chose c), go to question 17.

## 8 Do you like to:

**a)** work with your hands
**b)** build things
**c)** make music

If you chose a), go to question 19. If you chose b), go to question 11. If you chose c), you are **Peter Piper**.

## 9 Which would you prefer to do:

**a)** sword fight
**b)** play games
**c)** throw a fabulous party

If you chose a), go to question 11. If you chose b), go to question 14. If you chose c), you are **Prince Charming**.

## 10 Which is your favorite animal:

**a)** sheep
**b)** cow
**c)** dog

If you chose a), go to question 15. If you chose b), go to question 17. If you chose c), go to question 19.

## 11 How would you describe yourself?

**a)** large and powerful
**b)** clever and wily
**c)** tough and determined

If you chose a), go to question 16. If you chose b), go to question 22. If you chose c), go to question 20.

## 12 Do you prefer

**a)** lots of company
**b)** a few close friends
**c)** to be on your own

If you chose a), you are **Snow White**. If you chose b), go to question 21. If you chose c), go to question 15.

## 13 Do you prefer to:

**a)** sing
**b)** tell jokes
**c)** run races

If you chose a), go to question 21. If you chose b), go to question 19. If you chose c), go to question 9.

CONTINUED ON NEXT PAGE

**14** *Which is more appealing to you:*

**a)** shopping for shoes
**b)** going to the hairdresser
**c)** buying flowers for a friend

If you chose a), you are **Cinderella**. If you chose b), you are **Rapunzel**. If you chose c), you are **Beauty**.

**15** *What is your favorite color?*

**a)** black
**b)** white
**c)** can't make up my mind

If you chose a), you are the **Little Boy Who Lives Down the Lane**. If you chose b), you are **Little Bo Peep**. If you chose c), you are **Mary, Mary, Quite Contrary**.

**16** *Which do you like more:*

**a)** jewels
**b)** music
**c)** wrestling

If you chose a), you are a **Dragon**. If you chose b), you are a **Giant**. If you chose c), you are a **Troll**.

**17** *Which do you prefer:*

**a)** making music
**b)** going on an adventure

If you chose a), you are **Little Boy Blue**. If you chose b), you are **Jack and the Beanstalk**.

**18** *Are you a:*

**a)** sound sleeper
**b)** restless sleeper

If you chose a), you are **Sleeping Beauty**. If you chose b), you are the **Princess and the Pea**.

**19** *Do you like:*

**a)** city life
**b)** rural life

If you chose a), you are **Old Mother Hubbard**. If you chose b), you are **Old Macdonald**.

**20** *Would you say you have:*

**a)** great looks
**b)** nice teeth
**c)** commanding presence

If you chose a), you are the **Evil Queen**. If you chose b), you are the **Big Bad Wolf**. If you chose c), you are the **Evil Stepmother**.

**21** *Do you prefer to:*

**a)** help others in their time of need
**b)** protect others from danger
**c)** throw a good party

If you chose a), you are the **Fairy Godmother**. If you chose b), you are the **Blue Fairy**. If you chose c), you are the **Faerie Queen**.

**22** *Which do you like more:*

**a)** gold
**b)** orderliness and cleanliness
**c)** a marvelous dinner

If you chose a), you are **Rumpelstiltskin**. If you chose b), you are the **Farmer's Wife**. If you chose c), you are **Mr. Fox**.

GET YOUR ANSWERS RIGHT OVER HERE!

# So What *Is* Your Fairy Tale Personality?

## ABOUT THE CHARACTERS—AND WHAT THEY SAY ABOUT YOU....

### NAUGHTY -BUT NICE- CHARACTERS

In fairy tales, these characters are often portrayed as the "bad guys." But that doesn't make YOU evil, does it? Of course not! Like these celebrities of Happilyeverafter, you possess a love for the dramatic, a taste for adventure, and a flair for the larger-than-life gestures that bring certain stardom. Read about each individual character for a closer look at your superstar style and where it may take you.

### Big Bad Wolf

You're untamed all right, a "natural." Some people find you threatening because you don't hide your feelings. But you're an emotional type, and your emotions are big. Big laughs, big loves, big teeth. You'll fit right in on tour—as lead guitarist for the wildest band out there. Fans will love you (even if their grandmas won't) in "real" life.

### Dragon

You are hot, hot, hot! A shining star! A comet! Unfortunately for you, your over-the-top style is not always appreciated by regular folks. Some others even joke that seeing you puts them "in distress." Never fear—the catwalks of the high fashion world are waiting for you! Don those sunglasses. Pull out those jewels and baubles from your hoard of treasure. New York, Paris, Japan—they're yours. Go.

### Evil Queen

You know that pretty faces are a dime a dozen. To make it big, you need brains as well as beauty, and by golly, you've got brains to spare. So where can talents like yours find the widest scope? Hollywood, of course! You'll reign for years as the brightest light on the silver screen. Don't fret when younger, newer versions come along. You're a one and only.

### Evil Stepmother

You are ambitious and loyal. But you also have plans for yourself— big plans. And you have what it takes to make it happen: A fabulous design sense. So get out that tape measure, and flip through those home décor books. You can turn any old manor into a stunning palace that snobby Cindy would die for. Then do it all over again for your pals, and their pals, and their pals.... Next stop: A top-rated TV show of your very own!

### Farmer's Wife

Hard work is nothing to you. You have the stamina and endurance of an Olympic athlete. You also have excellent fine motor skills. Alas, you do have a bit of a temper. It gets a little out of control sometimes, especially when others try to steal the fruits of your labors. Zen breathing should help you stay calm under pressure—of which there is much in the operating room where you can put your talents to practical use. Best career choice: Hollywood Plastic Surgeon.

### Giant

Do you ever feel like a square peg in a round hole? That's the fate of giants like you. The good news is that your large size enables you to see "the big picture" and take the long view. You don't worry about silly concerns like manners. You get right to the heart of things. These traits, plus your love of unspoiled forest, make you the ideal environmental activist. Think green, big guy.

### Mr. Fox

You love the finer things in life: Luxurious linens, rich foods, top-quality soda. You also have excellent taste and can recognize quality at a glance. These skills will come in handy in a career as a food or film critic.

155

## Queen of Hearts

You are the diva of divas. When the spotlight is on you, you are truly royalty—generous to a fault, warm, loving, with a heart as large as the universe. No wonder everyone adores you in spades! Alas, sometimes, the stage lights go down, and the fans go home. Does this make you feel like shouting, "Off with their heads!"? Let it go. Starstruck fans will shower you with diamonds tomorrow. Best future career: Opera singer.

## Rumpelstiltskin

You figured out how to turn straw into gold. Cool! But being the clever sort that you are, you knew this was just the beginning of your rise to the top. A word in the right ear here, a little persuasion there, and the kingdom would be yours! You are a natural politician. Make the most of your talents by devoting yourself to public service. Just remember: Loose lips sink ships!

## Troll

Your height at times makes others underestimate you—but they do so at their own peril. You are as strong as they come. And with your quick wit and ability to solve any riddle in the universe, you are a powerful force indeed. Harness that strength and intellect and use it to make the world a better place. Your natural inclination toward bridges will help you bring warring parties together to bridge their differences. A career as a diplomat is waiting for you.

# THE ROMANTIC TYPE

You live for love, don't you? Ok, maybe not, but if it were up to you, life would be all unicorns and butterflies, rainbows, and lollipops. There'd always be a happy ending. Lucky for you—with your personality, you can make happiness happen!

## Beauty

You are not fooled by superficial appearances. You can spot a phony a mile away. So maybe this means you don't run with the most "popular" crowd. You know that the only person your friends need to be popular with is you.

## Blue Fairy

You make nice things happen. Just like when the sun comes out from behind a cloud, the mood in a room brightens the moment you enter. It's your warm personality that makes people feel good.

## Cinderella

Is there a bully or two in your life? Find an ally and you don't have to be a victim. Just remember that most bullies have problems of their own. Don't let their problems be your problems. Find a prince or fairy godmother for advice on how to deal with sticky situations before you miss the ball.

## Faerie Queen

If you were a musical instrument, you'd be a harp: Elegant. People enjoy being around you. They feel like something special is about to happen, that this will be a moment to remember. You take the everyday humdrum world and make it extraordinary. How? Who knows? It must be your own personal magic. Throw a party—a big one—soon.

## Fairy Godmother

You're very much the helper type. You help old folks cross the street, little kids who've dropped their toys, and moms who are wheeling heavy grocery carts. Keep up the good work!

## Princess and the Pea

You are one restless kid! Do you ever sit still? You're always on the move, out and about, going, going, gone! What do you think might happen if you slowed down for a moment? Took some time to watch a bird or a cloud? Give yourself some time to think, and to breathe.

## Prince Charming

Everyone wants to be liked, right? But do you go too far, pleasing everyone but yourself? You don't have to, you know. Be yourself. Whatever you do, some people will like you. Some won't. And that's ok—really!

## Rapunzel

You're a bit of a dreamer, and enjoy spending time on your own. Use your imagination to write stories, paint pictures, or compose music. You'll be amazed where your dreams can take you!

## Sleeping Beauty

It's hard for you to get motivated sometimes. Wouldn't it be wonderful if someone would just wave a magic wand and everything would just be taken care of for you—homework done, bed made, lunch packed? Maybe, but if other people do things for you, they will also control you. Wake up and look after your own life, sleepyhead, before it passes you by!

## Snow White

Do you ever feel like people are out to get you? Don't worry. You'll always find there are plenty of friends in your life to make up for the one or two rotten apples that are bound to cross your path. When you feel like life is closing in around you, and you're trapped, relax. Good times are just around the corner!

## MOVERS AND SHAKERS

You are the entrepreneurs of Happilyeverafter. You make the wheels of commerce go and provide the products that people use day in and day out. You have no patience for pie-in-the-sky romance—you want pie on your plate. And drama queens can go elsewhere—you've got a business to run, fields to plant, ideas to develop, money to make!

## Jack and the Beanstalk

You're the perfect business partner for Mary, Mary, Quite Contrary. You don't like taking direction from others, and have a strong interest in botany. But, unlike Mary, you are interested in trade, and are willing to change directions when new opportunities arise. Wall Street is the place for you!

## Jack Horner

You've heard that curiosity killed the cat, but that hasn't stopped you. You can't help asking questions and poking into things. You'll make a wonderful detective!

## Little Bo Peep

Patience is one of your greatest strengths. You know that if you are willing to wait, then most good things will come your way. Patience is especially important in businesses that require long-term investments, such as land development and tree farming. Consider purchasing a sheep farm in New Zealand.

## Little Boy Blue

You're a natural leader. You get everybody else up and on their feet, excited about the project. Use this terrific talent to found a company or to launch a new product. It's bound to be a success with you at the helm!

## Little Boy Who Lived Down the Lane

You have a good nose for money, and for what different items are worth. This talent means you will succeed in careers that involve buying and selling. Think: Real estate agent or stockbroker.

## Mary, Mary, Quite Contrary

You know your own mind and are not easily led by others. Combine this trait with a passion for nature, and you have the skills needed for a career in plant hybridization. You can develop new species of food and plants that can produce greater yields of grains and end world hunger. And what you could do with especially gorgeous and hardy breeds of flowers! Cockle bellflowers, perhaps?

## Old Macdonald

You have a knack for animals. They love you, you love them. Consider a career as a dog or cat breeder, a veterinarian, or a horse trainer. Of course, you can also have a farm or a ranch, if you prefer!

## Old Mother Hubbard

Your skills and interests lie in the domestic arena. You enjoy cooking and keeping a pleasant home for friends and family to enjoy. You also enjoy caring for pets, and bring efficiency and warmth to all of these areas. As a result, you are a pleasure to be around, and you will never be short of visitors!

## Peter Piper

Music is what turns your crank. You'd rather sing or play an instrument than just about anything, and would love to be a professional musician one day.

# ANSWERS

## page 8: WANTED: Reward Offered!

"B.B." Wolf, page 52; The Witch, page 48; Puss, page 23; The Farmer's Wife, pages 100 and 121; The Troll, pages 54 and 77; Jack, page 109; Queen Jelosia, page 30

## page 14: Wizard Spelling Bee

Wizard Walter of Wurmsen-Wurmsout: 6 spelling errors (onces/ounces, juce/juice, noot/newt, robbin/robin, untill/until, dun/done); Wizard Mathilda of Meinz: 6 spelling errors (tern/turn, serpint/serpent, perfuimed/perfumed, midnihgt/midnight, vile/vial, rezults/results); Wizard Dragon-breath of Hoboken, New Jersey: 3 spelling errors (clyent/client, televized/televised, Too/To); Wizard Tiffany of Primadonna: 5 spelling errors (protec-shun/protection, enslave-ing/enslaving, there/their, cliping/clipping, dayly/daily). The winner is Wizard Dragonbreath!

## page 24: "The Queen Is Not Amused" Puzzle

Three is the magical number in the code. Each letter in the royal names was *encoded* by

**158**

shifting 3 positions to the left (or *backward*) in the alphabet. For example, Q became N, E became B, A became X, etc. So to *decode* you need to shift each letter in the jumbled name tags 3 letters *forward* in the alphabet. It might help to write out the alphabet from A to Z and then underneath to write out the alphabet shifted 3 spots to the right as:

A B C D E F G H I J K etc...
D E F G H I J K L M N etc...

Now the letter sitting beneath the coded letter is the decoded letter (so A is D, K is N, etc.). Here are the coded tags and the decoded answers: NRBBK MORKX is **QUEEN PRUNA**; HFKD TFKDAFKD is **KING WINGDING**; IXAV IXCCX is **LADY LAFFA**; MOFKZB ELMXILQ is **PRINCE HOPALOT**; ARHB PEKLLH is **DUKE SHNOOK**; BXOI LC ZEBBPB is **EARL OF CHEESE**; PMLQ is **SPOT** (the dog).

## page 26: Fairy Tale Whodunit

Step-by-step solution:
• **Clues 1 and 2:** Since the dwarf is not wearing blue, red, or yellow, he must be wearing green. As we know the dwarf is in green, we also know he is not holding either the platter or lance, which means he is holding either the wand or the crown.
• **Clue 3:** The two objects made from a long stick are the wand and the lance. We know from earlier that the

dwarf is not holding the lance, so he must have the magic wand. As the jester is holding the other object made from a stick, he must be the one with the lance.
• **Clue 4:** Now we know that the dwarf has the wand and the jester has the lance. Since this clue tells us that Cindy does not have the platter, the only object left for her is the crown. And we now also know that the person with the platter is Prince Conman.
• **Clue 5:** Since Prince Conman is the one holding the platter, he is the person who is wearing red.

From the hidden camera picture taken in the Crystal Room, we know the thief was wearing yellow and carrying the lance. Now go back to what we learned at Clue 3: We know it's the jester who is holding the lance, which means he's the one in yellow. Since we also know the dwarf is in green and the Prince in red, it must be Cindy who's wearing blue. From the clues and the picture, we can now piece together everything we need to know about each person and their whereabouts: Cindy is the blue blur in the Throne Room, with the crown. The dwarf is in the Kitchen with his wand and wearing green. The prince is in the Great Hall, wearing red and helping himself to the platter of fish. And the jester, dressed

in yellow and carrying a lance, is the thief in the Crystal Room.

## page 30: Castle Scavenger Hunt

Clue #1: page 6; #2: page 10; #3: page 17; #4: page 27; #5: page 143; #6: page 147; #7: page 123; #8: page 120; #9: page 135; #10: page 93; #11 and #12, page 89

## page 36: Free Prince Valiant!

Princess Vitamina figured out that when the key is put into the dungeon door, a coin comes out with a number that is related to the first by the following equation: key number x 3 + 1 = coin number. For example, Mommy Valiant first chose the #5 key. 5 x 3 + 1 = 16, which was the number on the coin she received. This same equation works for all of the attempts listed in the log book (try it and see!). Vita figures out that if she needs a coin with the number 25 to free the prince, she must choose the #8 key, since 8 x 3 + 1 = 25.

## page 52: Lost in the Woods....

The solutions are: Wi**s**e Old O**w**l's Tree [choice of **s**outh or **w**est, choose west]; **S**now Whit**e**'s House [choice of **s**outh or **e**ast, choose south]; Han**s**el and Gr**e**tel's House [choice of **s**outh or **e**ast, choose south]; B**e**ast's Lair [choice of **e**ast or **s**outh, choose east (because south to Hu**n**ter's D**w**elling only gives you the option of **n**orth—back to where you came from—or **w**est, which is a dead end)]; **W**olf's Cro**ss**ing [choice of **w**est or **s**outh, choose **s**outh]; Old Crow's N**e**st Pass [choice of **w**est or **e**ast, choose east]; D**w**arfto**w**n [choice of **w**est or **n**orth, choose north]; **W**itch Haze**l** Hollow [choice of **w**est or **e**ast, choose east]. You made it to the Jolly Miller's Inn!

### page 54: Stump the Troll!

"I go through the mud": A wheelbarrow. "Little Nancy Etticoat": A candle. "The land is white": A book. "Thirty white horses upon a red hill": Teeth and gums. "He went to the woods and caught me": A splinter. "In marble walls as white as milk": An egg. "Two brothers we are": A pair of shoes. "A shoemaker makes me shoes without leather": A horse. "Old Mother Twitchett has just one eye": A needle and thread.

### page 62: Dear Fairy Godmother

"Sad, Sad Cindy" is Cinderella. "Little Pig" is the third pig (the one who built his house of brick) from the story of *The Three Little Pigs*. "Disgusted" is from the Mother Goose rhyme "Sing a Song of Sixpence;" the Pieman is the one

Simple Simon meets going to the fair in "Simple Simon Met a Pieman." "Feeling Like a Heel" is the "Old Woman Who Lived in a Shoe." "Rumbly in My Tummy" is the "Old Woman Who Swallowed a Fly."

### page 106: Picture These Words

1–B Answer: Jack

JACKET + TENT + KL – KETTLE + KO – KNOT

(**JAC**~~KETTENTKLKO~~ = JACK)

2–C Answer: Mother

MARCH – ARCH + COT + HERS – CS

(**M**~~ARCH~~**C**O~~T~~**HERS** = MOTHER)

3–D Answer: Army

ARM + KEY – KE

(**ARM**~~KEY~~ = ARMY)

4–A Answer: Roast beef

ROWBOAT – BOW – T + ST + BEE + F

(**RO**~~WBOAT~~**ST**~~BEE~~**F** = ROAST BEEF)

### page 110: Help Humpty!

Here's the completed egg, showing how the pieces fit together to make Humpty whole.

### page 111: Even More Fun with Humpty

See which shapes make each of the characters shown on page 111:

Goosey Goosey Gander

Blackbird

Cock Robin

Cock-a-Doodle-Doo

Poll Parrot

Swan

Crow

### page 116: Loosey Goosey's Hinky Pinkys

The mess in the chicken pen = coop poop; security for the barn = farm alarm; dog's bark = hound sound; magical being who milks cows = dairy fairy; portly puss-in-boots = fat cat; hag who's a tattle tale = witch snitch; fire-breathing lizard's cart = dragon's wagon; ailing fowl = sick chick; nearby lollipop = handy candy; goofy goat = silly billy; married rodent = mouse

spouse; clever song = witty ditty; seat for a bunny = hare chair; hairpiece for porky = pig wig; eager royal = keen queen; swamp of spaniels = dog bog; plump primate = chunky monkey; ill-behaved boy = rude dude

### page 118: Baa Baa Brain Teasers

**The Magic Carpet**

**Twinkle, Twinkle Little Star**

The largest number of squares with the yellow star in the center is 8.

**Grandma's House Puzzler**

### Seven Dwarves Challenge

Dopey + Bashful + Doc = Happy

Plug in what you know: 0 + ? + ? = 4

Since we know Dopey is 0 and Happy is 4, Bashful and Doc must be 3 and 1 (they couldn't both be 2, so that leaves only 3 and 1 to add together to make 4). But we don't know yet which is 1 and which is 3.

Dopey + Doc + Happy = Sleepy

Again, plug in the numbers you know: 0 + (3 or 1) + 4 = ?

Once again, we already know that Dopey is 0 and Happy is 4. Since the highest number any dwarf can be is 6, Doc must therefore be 1 (because if he was 3, the equation would add up to 7, which isn't possible). So in this step we learn that Doc is 1, which makes Sleepy 5. And going back to the first one, since we now know that Doc is 1, that means that Bashful must be 3.

Dopey + Sneezy + Happy = Grumpy

0 + ? + 4 = ?

We've already assigned the numbers 0 (Dopey), 1 (Doc), Bashful (3), Happy (4), and Sleepy (5) based on the earlier equations. Since we know from this equation that Grumpy must be higher than 4, Grumpy must be 6 and Sneezy 2, which works out (0 + 2 + 4 = 6).

Answer: Dopey = 0, Doc = 1, Sneezy = 2, Bashful = 3, Happy = 4, Sleepy = 5, and Grumpy = 6

## page 130: Mother Goose Trivia Quiz

1–b) 2–b) 3–c) 4–c) 5–b) 6–c) 7–b) 8–b) 9–b) 10–a)

## page 134: This Is the House That Jack Built…

• there's water instead of grass on the lawn, and grass instead of water in the pool

• the weather vane is mounted on the side of the chimney, not vertically

• fireplace is on the outside of the house, and on a different wall from the chimney

• there's a window over the fireplace

• curtains are hanging on the outside the window, not inside the house

• there are three windows of the same size but all have different panes

• there is a door on the second floor without stairs leading to the ground

• the garden is enclosed by an upside down picket fence

• there is no gate in the garden fence to give access to the garden, even though the front door is there

• the well has a shovel hanging from the rope, not a bucket

• the front door has hinges on the same side as the door knob

• the front door lights point in opposite directions

• the swimming pool ladder was installed from an upstairs window instead of the balcony

• stairs lead up to the garage door so a car can't go into the garage

• the house number on the garage doesn't match the number at the front door

• the swimming pool fence is mismatched

• the diving board for the pool is out over the ground, not over the pool

• there is no glass in the dormer window

• the window box below the dormer window has birds instead of flowers in it

• the shingles on the roof are slices of bread

## page 140: Wee Willie Winkie Map Quest

Collected letters spell out: "You snooze, you lose!"

## page 146: The Three Wise Men of Gotham

It is not advantageous to place the sum total of your barnyard collections into the same wicker receptacle = Don't put all your eggs in one basket. A chronic disposition to inquiry

deprived the domestic feline of its vitality = Curiosity killed the cat. An excess of culinary experts impairs the quality of a thin boiled derivative of meat = Too many cooks spoil the broth. Never situate the conveyance forward of the perambulatory equine = Don't put the cart before the horse. We will traverse that structure erected to afford passage over a watercourse at the occasion of drawing nigh unto it = We'll cross that bridge when we come to it. Refrain from enumerating your poultry prior to their incubation and emergence from their embryonic habitat = Don't count your chickens before they hatch. There's no value to be derived from demanding attention by loud screeches over fallen white liquid obtained from the lactic glands of a female bovine = There's no use crying over spilled milk.

Buh-bye